Praise for Bill Graves'
On the Back Roads—Discovering Small Towns of America

"...Graves descriptively captures the essence of
towns that boast bizarre claims to fame. Readers
will warm to his easy-going nature."
—Publisher's Weekly

"Never cute or sentimental, Graves writes with a
straight-ahead style that is immediately engaging and as
hard to step away from as a rambling fireside chat
with newfound campground neighbors."
—Los Angeles Times

"I picked it up, began to read, and hated to
stop for food or drink."
—America Online Family Travel

"A top-notch word picture of life and times
of charming small towns...his descriptions of the
intriguing people he meets along the way...makes this
a book that needs to be on your travel-book shelf.
—KKGO Radio Los Angeles

"an entertaining and sometimes touching narrative
of people and places..."
—Universal Press Syndicate

ON THE
BACK ROADS...

ON THE
BACK
ROADS

Discovering Small Towns of America

Bill Graves

Pati,
Perhaps someday you
will fill in the blanks
on the years I missed
with Patsy.

Bill

Addicus Books, Inc.
Omaha, Nebraska

5/25/08

An Addicus Nonfiction Book

ISBN# 1-886039-36-4
Cover design by Jeff Reiner, Josh Doolittle
Typography by Linda Dageforde
Cover photo–Sutter Creek, CA by Henry Mace
Back cover photo by Christopher Graves

Library of Congress Cataloging-in-Publication Data
Graves, Bill, 1933-
   On the back roads: discovering small towns of America / Bill Graves.
    p. cm.
   "An Addicus nonfiction book"—T.p. verso.
   ISBN 1-886039-36-4 (alk. paper)
   1. West (U.S.)—Description and travel. 2. West (U.S.)—History, Local. 3. West (U.S.)—Biography. 4. Cities and towns—West (U.S.) 5. Graves, Bill, 1933-   —Journeys—West (U.S.)   I. Title.
F595.3.G73 1999
917.804'33—dc21
                                 98-42821
                                     CIP

Addicus Books, Inc.
Web site: www.AddicusBooks.com

Printed in the United States of America

10 9 8 7 6 5 4 3 2

For Judy, Chris, and Kathy,
And for Connor, whose journey has just begun

Contents

Part V   Wyoming — Utah

Part VI   Arizona — Colorado — New Mexico

Acknowledgments

I wish to acknowledge residents of the towns that I visited who went out of their way to help me and point me in the right directions. And those generous nomads I ran into in campgrounds who drove me around, often to their favorite haunts, or tossed me their car keys saying, "Just bring it back in one piece."

I'm also grateful to the fine folks at *Trailer Life* and *MotorHome* magazines, especially Barbara Leonard and Bill Estes, who bought my first travel story. Later they went out on a limb with my idea for a monthly feature, "America's Outback,"—travel stories about places where nobody goes.

Most of all, I am grateful to some wonderful friends Marty and Jim Gamble, Barbara and Dave Hart, and Jeanne and Nick Mowlds. They provided me a fixed base and a roof over my head whenever I needed it, support, and encouragement, which I was in need of constantly.

Introduction

I told my friends, when I was writing this book, that it was about a former naval officer who could not stand the stress of retirement and ran away in a motorhome. Looking back, that is a pretty good description of it. It's honest anyway.

A few years ago, I was facing huge decisions, but from the perspective of a 22-year-old just starting life. I had no real job, no place to live, my kids were grown and doing well in the world, and I was single again. The difference, of course, is that I was older, maybe wiser and had an income. I did what I have never done before: I followed a dream. I took off in a motorhome to explore the West. I did not know where I was going—and didn't care much—but quickly realized that a destination is not important. The journey is what it's all about. For me it was everything—all there was.

I hung out where I felt like it, usually in the small towns that were a long way from the big ones. I may have missed some of the spectacular national parks and fun places average Americans go; and I may have missed a chance to meet tourists from around the nation. But that's okay. I was out there searching for that special breed of American who makes his life in the tiny towns of the American West, and I wanted to do it on his turf.

During many months of roaming the back roads , I was able to fufill that wish. And now, I am pleased to introduce you to the many fascinating people and places that were part of my unforgettable journey.

My motorhome helped make it all possible. It is completely self-contained right down to an electric generator that runs everything including my microwave and two air conditioners. It is comfortable, of course, but that is not what the motorhome lifestyle is all about—at least for me. It is about the independence and freedom that it offers, the absolute in free-spirit travel. Not ever tied to a schedule, a reservation, or even a clock, I let my curiosity run everything. I didn't have to read a sticky menu before breakfast or unpack a suitcase for my toothbrush. The motorhome did, and still does, offer life on my terms on the open road. And it doesn't get much better than that.

Two roads diverged in a wood, and I—
I took the one less traveled by,
And that has made all the difference.
Robert Frost
1874-1963

Part I

Southern California — Nevada

1

Emmy

Southern California Desert

Emmy was alone, camped a ways off the county road. If I startled her, approaching unannounced, she said nothing, except to politely offer me a chair.

Nearby, a shallow wash that ran with winter rains two months ago was filled with lupine and wild primrose. To one side bloomed a desert lily.

"I haven't seen a lily here for at least eight years. Its roots go deep, still it rarely gets enough water to give us a flower," Emmy said, laying aside her reading.

The view out front was a calendar picture. April. Springtime in the desert. Three folding chairs plus a pair of collapsible tables, now covered with her books and my camera case, furnished Emmy's open-air parlor. Moving a chair on her way to get us some tea, Emmy commented that most of her visitors come in pairs.

Emmy was a schoolteacher. An exemplary one, I would guess. Teaching was her life. She quit twenty-two years ago—retired, really—and has never looked back.

Eighty-three now, Emmy has no family. She never married. She sold what little she had, which didn't even include a house, and bought this self-contained camper.

Emmy had clear plans for the rest of her life. It shall be a journey. A true journey, she says, no matter how long the travel, never ends.

"My curiosity runs everything. I tell people that it even writes my schedule and usually overbooks me. There's just so much to do." Half-smiling, Emmy shook her head in apparent frustration. "Unfortunately, God gives none of us time to do it all, but I'm pestering Him for an extension."

"Think you will ever settle down?" I asked.

"Do I have to?" Emmy put on the pleading look of a teenager. "I am settled. That's the point. Just look out there." Her hand swept the horizon. "It's breathtaking! No person could plant a more beautiful flower garden. And if someone did, you and I couldn't sit by it like we are and watch the sun move across it all day."

Five months of spring freshen Emmy's year. If there is such a thing as a blooming wildflower circuit, she is on it. Starting in the lower desert of California in early April, she moves next to the high desert, then to the Pacific Coast, ending at 14,000 feet in the Sierra Nevada Mountains in August. The rest of the year, she roams the back roads of the West. Wildflowers, she says, are her fascination; America's small towns are her passion.

"Believe me, the little communities of this country are its last real hope," Emmy insisted. "There is not much inspiration coming out of the big cities. Have you watched TV lately?"

"I try not to."

She moved her chair and faced me. "When I am in one of those little cow towns, like in Nevada or Montana, it recharges my optimism. Kids walking home from school say 'hi' to me. They don't fear a strange face. Would you believe it? There are still places in this country where it is OK to be friendly with a stranger.

"You would be amazed at the number of people, born and raised in the city, who move to small towns and start over." Emmy reached for a book on the table. "I was just reading this [John] Steinbeck book. Must be the third time. He wrote this in the late fifties." She found the page. "Listen to this: 'As all pendulums reverse their swing, so eventually will the swollen cities rupture like dehiscent wombs and disperse their children back to the countryside.' Now, that's exactly what's happening."

Handing me Travels with Charley, Emmy continued. "Some people think it's just my generation or yours. It's not. It's everyone who wants to escape what is happening in the city. Families are desperate to make something for themselves, something of value that doesn't need to be chained down. I have seen them, young couples poking around small towns on weekends. I talk with them. And the next year when I come back, they run the bakery or the library or have an office on Main Street.

"You know, the man who doesn't strike out and do what it is he really wants to do in life...well, he is missing life itself. People are realizing that more and more, I think."

Emmy paused, maybe thinking I had something to add. Then she asked where I hailed from.

"Guess I'm homeless. I'm a runaway." It was a facetious answer, of course, and that's the way she took it. Honestly, both were true.

Emmy turned and looked at my comfortable motorhome.

"Face it, Bill. You aren't homeless. You're a vagrant!" she laughed.

"Vagrant? As in nomadic? I guess I can live with that."

"Live with it!" Emmy was shaking a finger at me. "There are millions who would take your place in a flash. I meet them all the time. Being a curiosity—or should I be honest and say an oddity—they come by and want to talk, just like you have. I explain that I don't own an alarm clock or a phone. I tell them that the only thing I have to do today—or tomorrow, maybe—is to see what's over the next hill. That makes them want to cry," she joked.

Emmy sat quietly for a moment, and sipped her tea.

"No, you are very lucky, and so am I." She was looking out over the desert, thinking beyond what she was saying. "There is so much to see. Have you ever seen the wheel ruts made by the wagons on the Oregon Trail?"

"Not yet."

"You will. The roads you travel will lead you right to them. Most people think I'm nuts when I ask that. But can you imagine? Just think about it, what a thrill when they discover the ruts made by those wagon trains are really there. Yes, in a New York second they would take your place. Some will eventually get out here. A few, maybe. But for one seemly good reason or another, most never will. And that saddens me."

Emmy was not just an astute observer. She was very wise. I'm sorry that I left without telling her that. Nor did I tell her that she accomplished what all teachers aspire to but few achieve: She filled me with questions about my life and how I should be living it.

What did Emmy mean by "the last real hope"? What is happening in the small towns of this country? All I actually know about present-day America is what I see in the newspapers and on television. Emmy, it appears, is a far better source than either of those.

I want to see the real America for myself. I don't mean a senior-citizen tour, seeing it out of the window of a sight-seeing bus. If the wagon ruts are still there, I will walk in them. When the main-street diner opens in the morning, I will be there to share coffee with those who want to chat. I will sit on the steps of the courthouse, and maybe in a rocker with a family on their front porch. And I'll see the sun rise over a place, any place, as many times as I want.

I can't cover the whole country, but I have the time, the mobility, and pocket change to see the West.

Emmy's words are still with me, what she said about a true journey. It never ends. I must admit, I have not yet started mine. It's high time.

2

Pegleg Smith's Lost Gold Mine

Anza-Borrego Desert State Park, California

I found a place to spend the night near a grapefruit orchard off Highway S22. My headlights swept a registered historic marker mounted in a rock pyramid. This is great, a site of epic significance. I parked my motorhome near the marker.

I dragged out cocktail hour and dinner and forgot the marker until I was ready for bed. But I had to know. So I trudged out in shower shoes with a flashlight to read the plaque. It told of Pegleg Smith, "a mountain man, prospector, and spinner of tall tales. The legend about his lost gold mine has grown. Countless people have searched..." So much for epic significance.

I read somewhere that there are 1,070 of these historic markers in California alone. Waiting for sleep, I wondered how many there are between here and Canada, between here and the Mississippi, between here and Duluth. Did they tell of Lewis and Clark, of Martin and Lewis, of Mickey Mantle, of Mickey Mouse? What was next, over the next hill?

I awoke in the dark to a wild and frightening sound. It was the scream of a coyote. He was close. I got up and opened the door, the chilly night drifting in around my bare feet. I saw starlight, as much of it as I have ever seen, and a satellite, whirling by as steady as a lamp. What is not on earth is best seen from this desert. Perhaps a cowboy in Montana might argue with that. But I have never seen a night sky in Montana or anywhere else as crowded with stars as this sky over the California desert.

The coyote was slinking off in a patch of thorny mesquite with his fellows of fang, poison, stinger, and claw. I would not see him unless he wanted me to. Coyotes are cagey, conniving cowards. They have a lot of enemies. I am one.

Last year, a pack of them killed our family dog, the only pet my two children ever had. A lovable, spoiled, miniature poodle, he was good at licking faces, not defending himself. When he was attacked, he probably yelped. Nobody heard him, so no one went to his rescue. I know he died wondering why.

I sat in the doorway, listening to the gentle voice of the night. It had taken up the details and shadows of the day and had wiped the face of the desert to simple, uncluttered blackness. My mind was reaching back, deriving memories from the most remote of sources. Surprisingly, I was not pushing them away or shutting them out.

I looked at my watch, not for the time but for the date. It has been eighteen months and two days since my marriage of twenty-four years ended. Tonight, I am feeling at peace with myself for the first time since. Guilt. Remorse. Shame. Defeat. All those gut-wrenching pains that pile one on top of another during the collapse of what was once a life-time commitment. They are gone, at least for now.

I am seeing a universe of stars and feeling awed by it. Hearing the chilling scream of a coyote and feeling both anger and sorrow, as if for the first time. It is easier to separate the two now. Anger is simple to handle. Sorrow, an affliction of solitude, is not and never will be easy.

I am paying attention. This moment is important. For months, I have been a non-participant, existing as an uninterested spectator, while valued life experiences have passed like meaningless news clips. They flashed and disappeared for my lack of attention or interest. There are no reruns.

It's a wonderful journey, this life. I don't want to spend any more of it asleep in the back of the bus. It's not too late. It never is. A man becomes his attentions. It is all he has, or ever will have. His observations and curiosity make and re-make him.

Emmy said it best yesterday: The journey is what's important, the getting there. The poor sucker who misses it, misses about all he is going to get.

3

Fossils in the Desert

Borrego Springs, California

The next morning, my principal decision was which way to turn. To go east would send me back the way I came, across desert canyons on S22 toward the Salton Sea. Turning the other way, in minutes I would be in Borrego Springs. Beyond it lay mountains and the Pacific Coast north of San Diego.

On the map, Borrego Springs appeared as a town to be stumbled upon while you're looking for someplace else. Driving through it is not the quickest way to get anywhere. It's off by itself, surrounded into perpetuity by the 600,000 acres of the Anza-Borrego Desert State Park, the largest such park in the continental United States.

Residents, I discovered, call the park the "green belt," or their guarantee that "southern California" will never get any closer to them than it is right now. About 3,000 people live here. Most are retired. Another 2,000 are here just for the winter. Those who stay the summer hibernate, as 100-degree days are the norm. For many, the state park is the reason they visit. For others, the green belt is the reason they stay.

Borrego Springs is laid-back to the point that even a traffic light would be too disruptive. I doubt it will ever have one. The town center is a traffic circle. It has a controlling sign that asks nothing more of anyone than to yield.

Around his forehead was a bandanna streaked with sweat and red dirt. The same earth tones spattered his Suzuki T-shirt that fit him like a decal. The cutoff sleeves displayed the beefy arms of a vain weight lifter.

A petite lady behind the counter, wearing the brown smock of a park volunteer, was explaining to him that the upper three miles of Coyote Canyon were now closed to vehicles. "Habitat restoration," she cited.

"That includes my dirt bike?"

She said nothing, staring at him over the flat-topped frame of her reading glasses.

"I'm all for the habitat," he argued, "but ya let guys on horses go up there. So what's wrong with me on a bike?"

"How about fifty-two sensitive species of rare desert plants in the canyon? They need a vacation from you macho guys and your bikes and trikes and Jeeps," she said, smiling.

While this duel was playing itself out, I was studying the map, spread on the counter that we three shared. Since we had the counter in common, I didn't feel that I was interrupting. "How is it driving out of here over the mountain?" I asked.

They both mumbled something in body language like, "Good, we can change the subject."

"You have a couple of choices," the lady said, looking up.

He jumped in before she could finish. "It's worse coming down. Believe me, I wouldn't think twice about doing that— going up Montezuma Grade, I mean."

I believed him. He had the look of a gutsy guy who would not think twice about doing most things. He pointed to a wavy red line on the map. It began at Hellhole Flat and ran up the San Ysidro Mountains. It was Montezuma Grade, a 3,200-foot rise on a ten-mile stretch of twisted roadway.

"Banner Road is easier," the lady offered. "That's how I go, even though it's longer."

He thought for a few seconds. "You didn't know that road has 107 curves in it, I bet? The guy that drives the school bus told me that. He does that kinda stuff, counts the curves."

"I didn't know that," the lady replied, expressing genuine interest. "But I'll tell you what my garbage man told me. When he is on Montezuma Grade, he puts down those two iron lifters on the front of his truck just for protection."

The dirt biker grimaced. "God, I hate to even think about that. He's not driving a garbage truck. That's a lethal weapon, a medieval tank!"

"From the map, Montezuma Grade looks a lot more winding than Banner Road," I said.

"But there is a lot less of it. You are through it in six miles." The biker was making a final point: "And they just put up a new guardrail along there."

"Fine...I don't intend to use the guardrail."

The end. Since I didn't have to go over the mountain, I wouldn't.

I was inside the visitor center of the state park, actually a natural history museum. The windowless building is an architectural lesson in desert survival, taught by the animals that live here. Built in 1979, three of its sides are buried in the sand. The entrance faces north, always in the shade.

Rosemary McDaniel, another lady in a brown smock, invited me to the back. The research lab, lounge, and conference room that displays things the public never sees. She and her husband, George, are among the 100 park volunteers. The opportunity to work here and pursue their interest in natural history was the big reason why they moved to Borrego Springs when they retired. He was a veterinarian, she a schoolteacher.

"Now we are lecturers," Rosemary said. "I do animals. He does fossils."

The sun-bleached skulls of Peninsular bighorn sheep lined the shelves in the conference room. The mountains of the park are among the last refuges for these sure-footed climbers, known for their massive horns that curve backward in a spiral. Bones of earlier inhabitants lay there too: camels, zebras, and several horse species. A giant fossil zebra found in the park, Rosemary told me, has been discovered nowhere else on earth. To paleontologists here like George, who talk of time in epochs, the bighorns were recent additions. They migrated to North America over 10,000 years ago from Siberia. Their numbers have dwindled to just 3 percent of what they once were. An estimated 750 remain in the United States. About 400 live here.

Grazing, mining, homesteading, and all that settlers brought to the West began the decline of the bighorn. But the metropolitan sprawl of southern California spelled real disaster. Off-road vehicles, trespassing cattle, poaching in the 1960s and early 1970s, plus drought and disease have pushed the bighorn population here to the brink. Efforts are underway to reverse that, from removing wild cattle to building new water sources.

Heading back to the campground in the park, where I had plugged in my motorhome earlier, I walked the trail through an after-dark picnic area for sixty species of reptiles—the usual night predators—and an occasional mountain lion working the desert floor. I remembered what Rosemary said: "If a cat is allowed to roam around the edges of town at night, it has about a two-year life span."

Grapefruit and lemon trees grow beyond the campground. They are the only crops cultivated here, except for grass on the golf links.

4

The Search Begins for Main Street

Borrego Palm Canyon Campground

An hour before the sun set, it disappeared behind the mountains, triggering nesting instincts in the campground. Awnings twirled up into rolls. Fire pits filled with wood. Ice cubes tumbled into glasses. Kids appeared and asked, "What's for dinner?" Propane lamps began to glow. The faces of Tom Brokaw and Dan Rather flashed on TV screens. We settled in.

I poured a martini into a chilled coffee mug and stepped outside to meet the neighbors. They all had busy lives elsewhere. They had come to get away from the stress. All too obvious, since this was a young crowd, mostly couples, many with children. Some had brought toys—motorbikes, dune buggies, even boats. They were day-campers or weekenders, not full-timers like Emmy. As a rule, I think this crowd prefers developed campgrounds like this one in a state park because there are things to do and room to do it. They give "recreational vehicle" its definition.

A couple walking a shaggy sheepdog stopped to ask if I had any flashlight batteries. "Be happy to pay for them, if you can spare a couple," the man said.

Before long we had his flashlight working again. He was so grateful, he refilled my coffee mug to overflowing.

They resumed their walk. I tagged along. We never did introduce ourselves, but they called each other Jerry and June. Their dog was Billingsly. New residents of Chula Vista, California, they brewed coffee for a living, six days a week, at a Starbucks store.

We talked some about America's current fascination with fine coffee. I confessed that I could never spend three bucks for a cup, no matter how fine.

"Funny thing," Jerry admitted, "I can't either. Hopefully there are only a few of us, or I'm in the wrong business. When I was a kid, growing up in Montana, my folks would drive forty miles to save a buck. Everybody went to the next town to shop at Wal-Mart. In those days, you spent time to save money. Now, you spend money to save time."

"When all those people took their business to Wal-Mart," I asked, "what happened to the stores back home?"

"Some are still there, some aren't...I guess, really, most of them aren't." All went uncomfortably silent. I could even hear Billingsly's chain jingle as he walked.

Then Jerry said, "What you are asking—or what you are saying, really—is that we ran our local merchants out of business. That our loyalty was to the almighty dollar and not to our neighbors. Let's put it this way—and I am defending my folks here—their loyalty was first to their family. There were just so many dollars to go around. They went where they could get the most for them. OK?"

It was too dark to see Jerry's face. Perhaps it was just as well. I was enjoying my second martini and a relaxing walk. I did not want this conversation to get too agitated or thought provoking.

"Guess it's basic economics, the free-enterprise system at work," I replied, maybe the most innocuous thing I have ever said.

"Exactly!" Jerry almost shouted. "The town is still there. Main Street didn't die. There is a generation growing up there now—actually, my generation—renovating whole sections of it. Fact is, I'm really anxious to get back there to see it."

June spoke up. "Well, I grew up in the town that has the Wal-Mart and the fast-food places, too. They all came at once. Then came the people from California with tons of money to buy up ranches and drive up the price of everything. The merchants loved it, especially the real-estate folks.

"Frankly, the new people didn't make good neighbors. They stuck to themselves. They were almost invisible, a cultural black hole that added nothing. And they brought big-city ideas and got mad because we didn't want to change to accommodate them. Why leave a place for a new place, then try to make the new one like the old one? I never could figure that one out."

"Would you go back?"

"To visit? Sure. My folks are still there. But I don't know what we would do there," June admitted. With a grunt, she poked Jerry in the ribs. "They wouldn't know Starbucks from instant, right?"

We were close to my motorhome. I made a graceful exit. Jerry and June had hit the right buttons. Their timing could not have been better. They had convinced me. More then ever, I want to be there. I want to see for myself what is happening to the small towns of the West. All of them, with or without a Wal-Mart.

Charles Kuralt once described those communities: "where Third Street's the edge of town. Where you don't use turn signals, because everybody knows where you are going to turn. And if you write a check on the wrong bank, it covers you for it anyway." Those places where the highway enters town and becomes Main Street because it was there first. That's where I'm headed.

Out in the desert, where the lights of our campground faded into darkness, other life began to stir and remake itself.

5

Oh-My-God Springs

County Road S22, California

The gods were pushing me toward Salton City. Were I driving a car, it wouldn't happen. But my big motorhome has the aerodynamics of an orange crate. A strong wind usually works against me. Head-on it's bad, broadside it's worse. But today, "it was a following sea," as I used to hear in the Navy. The wind, combined with a slope in the road, was keeping me at a consistent thirty-five miles per hour, with the engine idling in neutral. At six miles to the gallon, it was a gift from the gods.

As if spooked by the image of sinking beneath the ocean, the gods left me the instant I descended below sea level. The free ride was over. The zero-elevation line runs almost due north and south just west of Salton City, near the golf course and Oh-My-God Springs.

The Salton City golf course can be seen from the road, but not easily. It blends into the desert, since that is what it is. It has no grass. What identifies it as a golf course, really, are the flags marking the nine holes on the brown greens.

Oh-My-God Springs is even less conspicuous than the golf course, but then it's a mile off the road. It's probably named for the first utterance of some bird-watcher who stumbled onto this seedy nudist hangout while looking for a great roadrunner. *"Oh my god! Will you look at that!"* was the full sentence, I'll bet.

Other than running around naked and lolling in a hole of hot-spring water that is condemned by the county health department, what else this crowd does depends upon whom you talk to. In Borrego Springs, I heard five different stories from three people. Actually, I don't think it's any den of iniquity, just a ghetto-resort without a landlord.

I made a turn that looked like the right one. It was one of those roads that, in the desert, is a road because it has been driven on more than once. It immediately dipped into a deep wash. Coming up the other side, there it was: a thermal oasis and a ragtag collection of old trailers, converted school buses, and random junk. Cars and pickups were missing hoods, bumpers, and occasionally a wheel. Seats had been pulled from some, maybe for a person to sleep on. Nothing appeared durable or permanent.

They looked to be an antisocial bunch. At least they had set up housekeeping a good distance from one another. I saw no activity. Nobody worked or wandered. They just sat in front of their crude quarters with no clothes on. It was hot, though. These people were in no way related to the organized nudists who spend family weekends at health spas and earn a living fully clothed the rest of the week. This scruffy bunch was a long way from earning anything.

This was a sight indeed, a site of insignificance. No stone pyramid with a historic marker at this spot. Just a weathered sign warning of a health hazard.

Tragically, I suspect the road ends here for some. I mean the big one, not the mere tracks in the sand on which I drove in, and fortunately, would drive out again. My good fortune was not just that I could leave but that I had a place to go.

I parked and walked to the thermal spring. It was surrounded with tall vegetation. Propped up on one side was a plywood windbreak. The hot water bubbling from the ground was diverted into a hole that someone had dug. Around the top, the hole was lined with flat rocks.

Gathered were a half dozen well-sunned people, some in the muddy hole, some sitting on the side. Everybody had long hair. Empty Old Milwaukee cans floated in the brown water. No clothes in sight. Not even towels.

An ample woman, half in the hole—I would guess her age somewhere between thirty-five and sixty years—was tracking me with sunken eyes even before I got there. No one else, though, seemed to care about the arrival of a newcomer. She asked me, "Do you know how to fix a tellyvision?"

"No, don't even watch it much," I replied.

"Well, I ain't watched a bit since Friday. Quit dead in the middle of The Flukes of Hazard."

One of the guys said quietly, "It's Dukes, Dummy."

"Well, it quit in the middle, and I'm after someone to fix it."

A head of hair moved from the side to the center of the hole. It was a husky fellow in his late thirties. His arms and hands were half the normal size. Waist-deep in the hole, he moved to the edge, bent over, and picked up a pack of cigarettes with both of his tiny, deformed hands. Tapping the pack on a rock just once, a cigarette popped out. He put it between his lips without touching it with his wet fingers. Using a butane lighter, he lit the cigarette in a single, fluid motion. He had this procedure down to an art form.

A man with his back to me turned his head my way. "Did ya bring the beer?"

"Forgot it," I said, assuming an honest answer wouldn't work.

"The guys in helicopters never showed, neither. We is gettin' really low."

Dummy said, "There ain't no helicopters. You thought that up, just like always."

"They was here...when was it? They brought us that whatever it was. We played that good shit-kickin' music you like. Remember? Where the hell was you?"

Dummy didn't answer. She was sinking in the hole.

"They promised they'd come back and bring some more." Pointing at me, he said, "I thought he was one of 'em."

He rose on one elbow to face me, surfacing multiple tattoos, "You sure you're not one of 'em?"

"Sorry!"

He studied me for the longest time, then settled back in the hole.

I drove to Salton City, depressed by what I had just seen. For centuries, people have gone to the desert to lose themselves. The desert makes it easy. It happens almost as a matter of course.

Unable or unwilling to play the cards dealt them, lost souls drift from one shuffle to another in a desperate search for better ones. For many, the hunt invariably ends here in the desert, where the days are warm and life is undisciplined, unpoliced, and simple. In the vastness of the desert, a man can walk away from life yet still never take that last step.

"There is always hope," you might say. But only if you look for it. The ghettos, the mud holes, the pits of the desert are filled with those who have quit looking.

6

The Story of the Salton Sea

Salton City, California

The windows at Johnson's Landing all face the Salton Sea. So does the bar. I took a stool between a lady and a couple of older guys. I was offered a Salton martini: a glass of beer with an olive. Too early. My breakfast had not yet settled. Besides, the fresh coffee smelled pretty good when I came through the door.

Beginning at 6:00 a.m., Dorianne Fries sees anything that happens around the lagoon in front, though not much ever does. She has been the morning waitress here for a decade.

One morning a while back, a pair of stretch limousines rolled up to the boat ramp at the lagoon. They got her attention. Dorianne was well into this story when I sat down, but she was nice enough to start over again for my benefit. No one here seemed to mind.

According to Dorianne, silt in the channel had made the boat ramp useless years ago, but that was of no interest to the modish bird-watchers who stepped from the limos. They opened the trunks and pulled out long-lens cameras. Without a word, they spread along the salt-encrusted jetties surrounding the lagoon. Hundreds of birds, their twiggy legs knee-deep in the briny water, were busy scooping up bugs. Their

brief excursion over, heads shaking in apparent disappoint-
ment, the bird-watchers returned to their limos and drove off.

"They saw not one blue-footed booby," Dorianne recalled. "That's it right there, supposedly." Leaning across the
bar, Dorianne pointed to a dog-eared page in a bird book,
which had pushed my coffee cup aside. Edie Dean, sitting on
the stool next to me, had retrieved it from somewhere. It said
that the blue-footed booby "is shaped somewhat like a fat
cigar with a pointed-at-both-ends look." Although the bird is
found mostly in western Mexico, the book reported sightings
in southeastern California, including here at the Salton Sea.

"How do you know that's the one they were looking for?"
I asked.

"Because that's what those people all come here to see,"
said Dorianne.

"Have you seen one?"

"Could 'ave! I don't know." Dorianne shrugged and
flipped pages of the book. Reading upside down, she had
driven a spoon into the drawing of a large white bird. Its
neck was looped like a sink drain. "It says heron, right? OK,
two birds over, the exact same bird is called a common egret.
Now, I ask you, which is which?"

A man seated a couple of stools over interrupted in a
raspy voice. "Who cares what they call 'em. Just look at 'em
all. Must be three generations of those big buggers crapping
on the dock right now."

Dorianne rapped the page with the spoon. If it had been
a knife, the page would already be shreds. "But how do I
know what I'm looking at, which bird it is, when the book
doesn't even know?" Frustrated beyond reason, Dorianne
moved down the bar with the coffeepot.

Something grievously wrong had been festering here for
a long while. The bird book had nothing to do with it. And
it wasn't the layers of bird dung messing up the dock, either.
Nobody has used it in years.

What distressed Dorianne and the other locals who sat
with me that morning was more ominous, more tragic. It
wasn't the birds so much as what they represented: the tag

end of better times, perhaps the last gasp of life for their beautiful desert sea.

Then, like tears, their story started to flow.

"You should have been here back when people came to fish. On weekends, this parking lot was so full of boat trailers we couldn't even get in here," Dorianne remembers. "And the Saturday night fish fries lasted into Sunday."

Edie got up again. This time she brought me pictures of men holding up big fish. "These are from the corvina derby we used to have every year."

Others at the bar told of hair-raising rescues on the sea when a sudden wind riled up its shallow waters. Looking out at the lagoon, they swapped sea stories until the birds had done what they do here every morning and had moved on.

Once billed as California's largest recreational lake, the Salton Sea is big. It is thirty-five miles long and nine to fifteen miles wide. Recreational is now debatable, at best. Technically, lake never was right because it has no outlet. Geologists instead qualify it as a sink.

At 232 feet below sea level, the Salton Sea is the collector of irrigation runoff from the sprawling farms of the Imperial Valley. It's also the dump for the disgustingly polluted New and Alamo Rivers, which originate in Mexico. Water leaves only by evaporation. The foul pollutants go nowhere. They collect.

The 110-mile shoreline of the Salton Sea once had long, sandy beaches spotted with South-Seas cabanas and beach houses. Weekend crowds of swimmers and water-skiers flocked to the water, which registers summertime temperatures of ninety degrees. Marinas filled with shiny new boats as quickly as slips could be built for them. Bathing-suit manufacturers staged national beauty contests here. Boat races and regattas drew excited and colorful crowds from as far as Las Vegas and Phoenix. Bing Crosby, Dean Martin, and other Hollywood stars dined at the beautiful Salton Bay Yacht Club. Its floor-to-ceiling windows looked out over the blue sea, the desert, and the Chocolate Mountains.

Offering exciting promise, the Salton Sea was a glamorous place in the 1950s and 1960s. Only 150 miles from Los Angeles, this 300,000-acre saltwater lake in a mountain-rimmed desert, was also a real-estate promoter's dream. The promoters moved here in 1958, creating a place called Salton City and began selling lots at $200 down. Responding to TV and radio ads, speculators flocked to the barren desert to scoop up the raw land. A million-dollar freshwater distribution system was built for a population of 40,000. Power lines and 265 miles of streets were laid out on the sand. Some were paved. Every intersection had a sign—as they do today—bearing the names of the empty streets.

Spread over 19,600 acres of flat desert, the seaside paradise was ready for a city that never came. In the late 1960s, the whole thing collapsed, as speculative land promotions often do. The promoters packed their tents and disappeared.

Today the Salton Sea is an ecological disaster. Irrigation runoff dumps 4 million tons of salt, plus fertilizer and insecticide residue, into the sea every year. At Salton City, a foul smell often hangs over its hard, salt-encrusted shores, washed by water that is the color of cloudy tea and 29 percent saltier than the Pacific Ocean. The rising water of the sea has claimed its beaches and marinas, their crumbling structures half submerged and covered black with barnacles. Hot desert air blows through the empty windows at the abandoned, bankrupt Salton Bay Yacht Club.

Obviously, the Salton Sea has had its share of bad press. CBS's 60 Minutes reported the New River has been dumping raw sewage into the sea for forty years and called it the nation's dirtiest. Local residents had hoped the 60 Minutes piece would wake up the political bureaucracy to the ecological tragedy happening here. It did just that. But it also ran off the fishermen.

Next to Johnson's Landing is the RV park where Curt Goodpasture lives. He has fished the Salton Sea for over thirty-five years. "Better than half my life," he says. "Fish aren't as big as they were. But all this talk about the fish being gone, it ain't so. It's serious fishermen that's gone.

These guys who come out now just like to drink beer in a boat."

People here grieve for their desert sea, but science and politics may yet save it. While they wait, life here is otherwise serene, unrushed, uncrowded, simple, and healthy. The sun's entry and exit behind the mountains is gorgeous. And so is the Salton Sea, best viewed from a little distance.

Salton City's population has remained stable at 1,050 for the last few years. Yet the bird population has grown considerably. Why? Maybe the bug population has grown, too. Then again, the birds may know something we have yet to understand.

7

Hunting for a Caboose

Interstate 10, California

The open road, like having time to kill, will prod a man's curiosity into running wild, once boredom has turned it loose. I was headed east on Interstate 10 with a rumbling pack of Peterbilts and Kenworths. Exhaust lids flapped with each gear change. Tied together by machinery pushing its limits, we made the long pull out of the Coachella Valley. We peaked at 1,705 feet, Chiriaco Summit. Reaching the straight and level, the pack unravels and scatters, never to remake itself.

All was peaceful, as boredom always is, until a sudden reverberating rumble brought me straight up in my seat. A train! Filling the side mirror, it appeared to be passing in the other lane. After four diesel engines dragged their thunder down the track, a trail of container cars banged along beside me. Our speeds were a close match.

Freight trains blend into the natural setting of the West like cattle. There are so many of them. But this train was not one with the landscape. It was too close and intimate. Like the pack of trucks, we were instant comrades, bound by a common goal in the desert: to get to the other side.

The caboose is the personality of any freight train. I was looking forward to seeing it. Maybe I would swap waves with the guys inside. I even slowed down to speed it up.

As a kid, visiting my Grandmother Sheakley in New Hampton, Iowa, a train whistle sparked a ritual. My cousins and I would race for the tracks to wave at the passing freight. A caboose was always the ceremonial ending, crowned with the guy in its cupola who always waved back. Ah, sweet memories!

This train ended with no caboose. I was a witness to an incomplete event, like a ball game with no ninth inning. Two more trains passed during the hour. The same flat ending.

This is not Iowa. It's fifty years later. Doesn't a transcontinental train still need a caboose?

The answer was not out here on the interstate. But I knew where to look. The Riverside County road map would be a good place to start. County maps show railroad tracks. Any town with a railroad going through it would do just fine. Someone there would have the answer. Such extensive map research, however, must be done over a counter with a cold drink in a cool place. Ahead was the exit for Desert Center.

8

Rest Stop of Wilted People

Desert Center, California

I coasted down the off-ramp and turned onto a road that led under the interstate. This was Desert Center, basically little more than a hard-sand parking lot.

The road goes on to Kaiser's Eagle Mountain Mine, which shut down years ago. People in Los Angeles want to dump their trash in the hole that Kaiser left, an idea, I later found, that is intensely unpopular out here.

A line of eucalyptus trees provides most of nature's shade here. Two motorists with overheated cars currently have the shade well occupied. Wearing minimal clothes, they don't move or talk. They just stand there, wilted, surrounded by water jugs. Their body language gave a temperature reading in human terms, easily read. It's hot, but it's not even summer yet.

Steady business at the Stanco gas station testifies to the success of Desert Center's leading industry. A short distance away is Stanco's predecessor, a deserted garage with a remarkably well-preserved look of the 1930s. I parked in front and quickly noticed how buildings age gracefully in this dry air.

Adjoining the old garage is the Desert Center Café. Behind the café lay what was once a swimming pool. I walked around it. On the ground behind a fence lay a collection of aged mining equipment. It had its own patina from years of use and exposure in the desert.

I pushed open the door of the café. How nice it was to be cool! I ordered a glass of ice tea and flopped three maps, my caboose-search source material, down on the counter. Two stools over, a young woman was counting and packaging a heaping pile of pennies.

Desert Center appears on the map of California as a town. In this desolate desert, it probably is a town, consisting as it does of an air-conditioned, twenty-four-hour café, a filling station, a small food store, a post office, four pay phones, and some shade.

I opened the Riverside County road map and my glasses and began looking for railroad tracks.

"Café ran out of pennies," the lady next to me volunteered. I suspect she felt compelled to explain what she was doing, although the scene was pretty self-explanatory. She went on to say that the closest bank was an hour away.

"Guess water isn't the only scarce item in the desert," I said.

Figuring now that she had publicly established her reason for being, she would concentrate on counting pennies.

"Oh, we never run out of water!" she snapped, as if I had insulted her hometown.

But it didn't end there. The pennies belong to her son. He is saving for a camera. The Greyhound bus stops in front of the café twice a day. She works the graveyard shift here. Her husband is a mason and commutes to Palm Springs every day. She was telling me all this and counting pennies at the same time. How, I don't know.

I located the railroad tracks, but I had to rustle open a second map to find out where they went.

"Everybody here works." She looked up at the waitress who was standing over me with the ice-tea pitcher and setting down a plate of monstrous lemon wedges. "Don't you think, Judy?"

"There is nothing else to do," Judy answered, refilling my glass.

I asked Judy about the old mining equipment by the pool.

"That belongs to the owner of the café," Judy replied. "You should talk to him. He is working at the gas station today."

I hesitated. "You mean he owns this place and works at the gas station?"

"He owns the gas station, too."

The lady with the pennies sealed a roll by thumping it on the counter. "His father really owns it, or the Ragsdale family, anyway."

"They own it all," Judy added.

"All?"

"Ya, what there is," Judy continued as she started for the kitchen. "What ya see is it."

The lady bagged her son's pennies and carried them across the room to the cash register. Judy accompanied her.

I studied the map and identified the railroad town. It's in the next county, 116 miles from here up Highway 95.

Getting up to leave, I decided my interest in the old mining equipment did not extend beyond the limits of the air-conditioning. The same could be said for the Ragsdale empire. By the door, however, a rack of caps caught my eye. The fronts read Halley's Comet, Desert Center, 1986. Did Ragsdale have a piece of the comet stashed somewhere? Guess I have to ask the owner.

Sweat trickled down my neck after the two-minute hike to the gas station. Sidney Ragsdale was pulling a crooked Coke can out of a dispenser. He was a husky, weathered man of about forty.

I asked about Halley's Comet and the mining equipment.

My manner? My questions? Something had brought up his guard. Perhaps I didn't fit the profile of the "average" stranger. Any man who spends his life serving the traveling public must develop a suspicion of people, at least a skepticism. Every kind of folk wanders in off the interstate. He has probably seen them all and has built up a mental data bank on the human animal to fit his survival needs.

"The Halley's Comet hats were my dad's idea," Sidney explains. "We had people by the busload come here to see it in 1986. Because the air is so clear out here and there are no city lights, it's a good place to watch for it. It only comes by every seventy-six years, like once in a lifetime." Still, something bothered him. "Are you from the county, one of those guys who wants to dump out here?"

"No, I don't need to dump." I wasn't sure what he was getting at, unless he was talking about the wastewater tanks in the motorhome.

"Where's your car?"

"I'm traveling in a motorhome. It's over by the café."

An eighteen-wheeler hid half of it. Whatever he saw was my ticket of credibility. Out here in the desert, perhaps a vehicle told Sidney as much about its owner as he needed to know.

"Give me a minute. I want to take you on a special tour." Sidney locked up the drink dispenser. We piled into his pickup, went back to the café, and into the back office.

The only thing new in there was a calculator. Once something was hung or stuck on the wall, apparently it never came down. A 1934 calendar pictured Desert Center on Highway 60. The caption read, "Our Main Street is 100 miles long."

Sidney grabbed some keys. We walked next door to the old garage. I noticed the pumps in front last pumped gas for thirty-four cents a gallon.

The garage was the size of a ballroom and crammed with memorabilia. It struck me as the ultimate fantasy storage shed of a desert rat. Treasures from yesterday lay in the shadows, gathering dust, dripping oil into delicate puddles on the concrete. An old-fashioned fire engine. An antique car with spoked wheels. What looked like a guillotine was really a cheese press, the oldest thing there. The newest was a mock-up of a train engine and tender used in the movie Tough Guys.

"The Disney people wanted to buy the mock-up for their theme park in Florida. Dad saves things, never sells them," Sidney smiled.

Three dusty motorcycles leaned on stands. One was a U.S. Army Harley-Davidson that General George Patton left here in 1942. A leather rifle holster that looked like it belonged on Wyatt Earp's saddle hung on the side. Patton's army trained in the desert here for the African campaign of World War II.

Unwritten history fills that old garage. I'll bet years from now, others will find things just as I have. Nothing will be disturbed, except maybe to make room for more memories.

9

A Day Dedicated to the Caboose

Needles, California

A couple of hours later, I was in Needles, California. The off-ramp dropped me in the center of town.

In front of me spread an imposing two-story building. It covers nearly a city block. Shaded by tall palm trees, it had a soothing, cool look. Its windows and doors were covered with weathered plywood marked with a spattering of graffiti. Despite this contemporary look nailed to it, the old concrete building had retained its ageless dignity.

Behind it, heat shimmered above rows of iron tracks that steel wheels had polished to silver.

The only person in sight rode a lawn mower around the parklike setting in front of the building. He worked around old shade trees and stately palms, a cannon framed by an iron fence, wooden benches, and iron light poles topped with white spheres. It was a picture out of the 1930s.

The sun was turning my aluminum roof into a radiating hot plate. I found a big tree and parked where the sun couldn't get at it. I got out, crossed the street, and walked through the scent of just-cut grass to read the brass plaque on the cannon. It was a memorial to those who died in "the World War." Obviously, when they engraved this, there had been only one. If the cannon fired, it would knock the sign off the old Sears Authorized Catalog Sales Merchant store.

The plaque, the cannon, the catalog store, everything was dated, refreshingly outdated. Insanity to renovate has not yet destroyed this place. Perhaps it never will.

The door to the nearby senior center was open, so I wandered back across the street. The senior center lay adjacent to the dirt lot where my motorhome was parked. At the front desk, a lady with a pencil stuck in her hair finished a phone conversation about bingo. I asked about "the train station." My first mistake.

"It wasn't a train station. It was a Harvey House."

I asked if the Harveys still lived in town.

Both of her hands hit the desk. Her voice rose an octave. "My goodness! You don't know what a Harvey House is? It was a big chain of fancy restaurants. They had places all over the country."

Fortunately, the phone rang. Someone at the truck scales on Interstate 40 had ninety bags of onions for the seniors. She said that the senior center gets a lot of free produce off over-weight trucks.

"The Harvey House has been closed for years now," she continued. "They want to tear it down, but the city wants to save it. So there it sits. Something to look at, isn't it?"

I got around to the caboose question. She pointed out the office of the Burlington Northern–Santa Fe next to the tracks.

John Myers, a railroad employee, waited for a train to come in from the east. His crew would take it 145 miles across the sweltering Mojave Desert to Barstow, California. There, another crew would run the train down Cajon Pass to San Bernardino. He would spend the night at the Cool Water Motel in Barstow, as he has hundreds of times. The next day, his crew would bring another freight train back to Needles.

All trains of the Burlington Northern–Santa Fe change crews in Needles. That's the way it has been for decades, twenty-four hours a day, every day.

At John's feet rested a small nylon bag. Not completely zipped shut, work gloves and a walkie-talkie stuck out of the top. He has been a brakeman for twenty-four years, though he looked very young.

He and the others who entered and left the office wore no special outfit that identified them as a train crew. No red neckerchiefs. No black-and-white striped caps. They could easily have passed as electricians or ranchers going about their work here in Needles on any 100-degree day.

We talked about railroading. I asked my caboose question as if it were an afterthought. I didn't let on that I had dedicated my whole day to his answer.

"I think the caboose went off the line sometime in 1986. You will still see one now and then, but it's rare. I would say 99 percent of the freight trains have no caboose now," John said.

"Do you miss the caboose? Wasn't it like a lodge for the royal order of trainmen?" I was searching for something that only a veteran railroad man might feel. Ask an "old salt" about his early days at sea, and his eyes usually glaze over with time-embellished memories.

I was watching John's eyes. He was only looking at his watch.

It was not going to happen. John apparently had no tales of the good ol' caboose days. Maybe there were none. Or maybe they were before his time, like back in the 1940s in Iowa.

A five-engine train squeaked to a slow stop. The rest of John's crew, a conductor and an engineer, came out of the freight office with their bags of clothes. One carried a heavy ice chest, the other a handful of computer printouts.

We walked to the train together.

The other crew was climbing down from the cab one by one, handing bags down to one another. John's crew hopped aboard immediately. There were no handshakes or greetings normally expected when travelers come home or leave. There was no discussion between engineers, as you might expect when the helmsman is relieved. No conversation at all. It was as unceremonious as the changing of shifts in a steel mill.

The first engine began to roar. The train started to move. I felt its thunder in my gut. The rest of the engines picked up the throb until they roared in unison.

In less than a minute, the train was gone. All was still. I was standing in the sun. Just me. It was hot.

10

El Garces: A Harvey House

Needles, California

"You in there?" She yelled through my screen door. It was the lady from the senior center with the pencil in her hair.

I approached to the door. "You looking for me?" I asked.

"Sure am. That is, if you want to know about the Harvey House. A couple of people at the center know all about it. Plus I've got some onions for you."

"I'll be there," I said, "but how did you find me?"

"This is a small town," she replied and walked away.

Seemingly, that was all the answer I needed, or at least all I would get.

I was about to open a beer and let the remains of the day just play out. Small town or not, since she had made an effort to find me, I would go. Besides, I knew it was cooler there than in my motorhome.

Harvey Houses, named for their founder Fred Harvey, who died in 1901, were spaced a meal apart along the route of the Santa Fe Railroad from Kansas City to Los Angeles. Before the days of the dining car, cross-country passengers on the Santa Fe took all their meals in Harvey Houses. Built in 1908, the one here in Needles was named "El Garces" after

Father Francisco Garces, a missionary who came to this area in 1776.

"Indian women, arms covered with strings of beads, were always on the platform hawking their wares, day and night," remembers Pete Jewell. Pete has lived here for sixty-five years and has worked for the railroad forty-eight of them. "Near the end, when the trains stopped only for a five-minute crew change, passengers would get off to stretch and buy from the Indians. By the late 1950s, the Indians stopped coming. Couldn't sell much to a freight train."

Pete remembers El Garces in its prime. "Everyone ate on linen-covered tables with fine china. Fresh flowers were on every table. The ice-cream and soda-fountain room is still there. The walls are all marble. Made it cooler in the summer. Nobody has touched it, except for the pigeons. They have nested in there over the years and have redecorated it a bit. The waitresses, they called them Harvey Girls, all lived there too. They were farm girls, recruited mostly from the Midwest."

Jo Brochheuser was a Harvey Girl. "My number was seven. We all had numbers like football players. We wore two-piece white uniforms and hair nets. The top had a high neck and long sleeves. I remember, vividly, washing those uniforms in a big washtub and then starching and ironing them. How do you forget that?

"In the summer, when it was really hot, they would bring in a boxcar loaded with ice and blow the cool air into the sleeping rooms with big fans. The coolness reached the whole building."

By the mid-1940's, passenger trains had dining cars. El Garces became a dormitory for train crews and section workers until it closed in 1950.

With twilight coming on, I walked across the lawn in front of El Garces. I suppose the trees are taller, but everything now is as it was: the benches, the cannon, the soft light, even the air, heavy with heat. It was not hard to imagine this magnificent place three-quarters of a century ago, alive with anticipation and hope. Passengers strolling along the platform, maybe drinking a soda or eating ice cream, or just sitting here on the cool grass while the train took on what it needed for the last leg of its trip to Los Angeles.

I crossed to my motorhome, where neglected grass had been sucked dry by the sun. The grass was stiff and brown. It crunched under my feet like corn flakes, a reminder that this is a desert.

Nearby, six fifty-gallon drums were in their final days of supporting a dilapidated wooden platform. Its railing already lay on the ground. I imagined it was once decorated with flags on the Fourth of July.

Just like the caboose, El Garces was useful once, even important.

11

The Last Boomtown

Laughlin, Nevada

The individual was supreme. The gold in his britches often determined just how supreme.

They were the ultimate fortune seekers. Whether a gold miner or a merchant on main street, each man was betting on his ingenuity and his skill, or maybe just that his back would hold up. It was every man for himself. No corporate conglomerates or government agencies were making rules or exacting a piece of the action. No special interest groups shouted demands. In fact, demands of any kind were usually ignored, if anyone was brave enough or silly enough to make any. When an entrepreneur came to town, his competition and his bankroll were the only considerations as to when and where he set up business.

They made the boomtowns of the West, those tent cities that sprung up overnight in Nevada and the gold country of California beginning around 1850. They were the purest form of free enterprise this country has ever known. We have not seen the likes of them for about a hundred years.

Many wild, often lawless boomtowns grew quickly into first-class cities of thousands of people with newspapers, banks, churches, breweries, fancy hotels, and opera houses.

The appetite of their founders for instant riches and adventure was insatiable. They were always on the move. Miners moved to the newest discovery when the one they were working played out, if it ever produced at all. The camp followers were close behind. Some of the towns disappeared, but most are still around in an abbreviated form. Those days are history.

The craze for uranium ore created a few little boomtowns in the West in the 1950s. Oil discoveries made some before that, and some later in Alaska, but they were a different breed. Big money created them, not free spirits. Those towns were laid out on drafting tables, not lined off in the dirt with a stick. They were proper company towns where everybody knew who the boss was. An infrastructure was always in place and expanded as the town grew.

The last boomtown of this century, maybe the last one of all time, is in Nevada. It is probably the only state where it could happen. Laughlin, now the second-largest gambling mecca west of the Mississippi, has a workforce of 14,000 people. Eight thousand people live here. Another 50,000 visit every weekend. In 1984, the population was 95. When Neil Armstrong walked on the moon in 1969, the town of Laughlin was just a year old.

What is nostalgic, even exciting, about this place is that it has grown with the same mania and madness that characterized its true predecessors. Laughlin has never had a mayor, a police force, or town infrastructure. A county commission that is nearly a hundred miles away still governs it. It still borrows its cops from the police department in Las Vegas. There was such a rush to put up casinos and hotels, nobody waited for adequate roads or proper traffic control. Parking space was never a problem in the empty desert. Getting to it was.

For many years, Laughlin had thousands of hotel rooms but not one hospital bed. It had dozens of gift shops and bars, but no library, schools, churches, parks, not even a jail. Today it has some of those things, plus a lot more hotel rooms—11,000 that are occupied 93 percent of the time.

As a boomtown, it's a hybrid. It was built with corporate money, yet its genesis was with a latter-day pioneer named Don Laughlin. By definition, it sprung up "overnight," but not due to an oil gusher or gold strike. If there was a "discovery" at all, it was that conditions and times constantly change in this country.

Laughlin, located at the bottom tip of Nevada, sits right on the Colorado River across from Bullhead City, Arizona. In the early years, there were two ways to get from Bullhead City to Laughlin: by shuttle boat, operated by the casinos, or by driving up the river and crossing on Davis Dam. Obviously, that drive was an inconvenience for customers, a condition casino operators abhor. Gamblers are not gambling when they are driving. The boomtown needed a bridge.

Rather than wait for two state and two county governments to decide where a bridge should be located, casino owner Don Laughlin built one where he wanted it and then gave it to them. It cost him $3.5 million. Generous? Sure, but cleverly so. The 745-foot span is right next to his property— his roulette tables, poker games, and a couple thousand clinking, chiming, chrome-plated slot machines that take everything from nickels to twenty-five dollar tokens. Don Laughlin's Riverside Resort Hotel and Casino gets first crack at the gamblers pouring into town across his bridge.

I left Needles at 8:00 this morning, crossing from California into Arizona and into a later time zone. An hour later, I crossed Don's bridge, leaving Arizona and entering Nevada. Now I am back in the earlier time zone. So I get to pass through the nine o'clock hour twice this morning. It's great how these magical things happen on the road.

I turned into Don Laughlin's 800-site RV park across from his casino complex. It is Sunday and very busy. I have stayed in Laughlin many times, but it grows so fast, each time is a visit to an updated version. I have met Don before, but I am going to look him up again.

Don lives in a rooftop penthouse over the twenty-eighth floor of a new wing of his 1,404-room hotel. A lady in his office told me that Don does not show up there until late in the morning. He usually works after midnight, especially on Saturdays. I arranged to meet him later at the tea dance, a Sunday-afternoon tradition at the Riverside, where Don is a regular.

Don started here in 1964, when he plunked down $35,000 for a small bar and restaurant on six acres of land next to the river. Called the Riverside, it had twelve slot machines and was on a brush-lined, dirt road that led nowhere. "When it rained, the road was one long mud puddle," recalls Danny Laughlin, who grew up in the town named for his father.

Although Don's contribution is deserving of the town being named after him, he claims that it was not his idea. Relaxing at a table in the ballroom between dances with his girlfriend (he is divorced), Don explained, "A lot of people look at it like, boy, you must be on a big ego kick. You got the town named after you. My answer is jokingly, 'No, they named it after my mother.' "

He had wanted to call the town Riverside or Casino, imitating another Nevada border town named Jackpot. But the people at the post office changed his mind. "The man who came down here was named O'Neil," Don explained. "I forgot his title. Postal inspector, I think. He said that they didn't like my suggestion of Riverside or Casino because they are too common. He said Laughlin was a good Irish name. O'Neil liked it, so that's how it happened."

The son of poor farmers in Owatonna, Minnesota, Don knew early on that he didn't want to be a farmer. Although gambling was illegal in Minnesota, many people, including his mother, played slot machines. They fascinated him. Don bought his first one out of a mail-order catalog. Until his high-school principal came down on him, he was taking in more money as a student than most full-time workers in Owatonna. So he quit school to operate his six machines, placed in taverns and stores, until Minnesota stopped turning a blind eye to gambling.

Don moved to Las Vegas in 1952 at the age of twenty-one. Finally in his element, he worked as a bartender and went to dealer's school at night. Don saved his money and two years later bought a bar and restaurant. He sold that after ten years, moved here, and made a boomtown that never closes.

Don is probably many times a millionaire. What's important, he's doing what he wants to do with his life and very much on his terms.

He flies his own airplane and keeps a helicopter tied down just outside the back door of his casino. He works all the time but relaxes by walking through his spacious casino, usually eating a bag of popcorn. He is not a big guy. He blends in easily with his customers. Though few people notice him, he is under the constant surveillance of the casino security cameras. They track his every move. After all, he's the guy who can open the safe.

12

Highway 95:
450 Miles and One Traffic Light

Beatty, Nevada

B uilt originally of rock, layered with wood ties and steel
rails, today it's asphalt. U.S. 95 through the Amargosa
Desert lies on the roadbed of the old Las Vegas & Tonopah
Railroad. Between 1906 and 1918, it carried trains of gold and
silver and the equipment to mine them. Now it's cars, trucks,
and tour buses filled with a geriatric crowd on a free ride to
a Las Vegas casino.

There must be fifty small towns between here and Canada
where this highway is Main Street. Goldfield in Nevada. Jor-
dan Valley in Oregon. Craigmont in Idaho. It's the lifeline for
many small towns of the West. U.S. 95 continues into British
Columbia, where it becomes the Crowsnest Highway.

Open Range signs along here are not the common black-
on-yellow profiles of startled cows. They are the silhouettes
of horses or burros, both of which run wild in the Nevada
outback and number in the thousands.

Over the Funeral Mountains to the west and down some
3,500 feet is the immense, scorching floor of Death Valley.
Ahead is a dump for low-level hazardous waste that is

trucked from as far away as Texas. The dump once took in radioactive leftovers, but not anymore.

In the mountains to the east and north is the Nellis Air Force Range, so my new map says. The old one, which I just threw away, included the words Bombing and Gunnery in the name of this 3-million-acre facility. I question motives when a government changes place-names for no apparent reason. Obviously, bombing and gunnery are still what go on there, because that's what the Air Force does.

The Nevada Test Site begs the same skepticism. The word Nuclear was in that name originally, back in the testing heyday of the Cold War. Between 1951 and 1958, the Atomic Energy Commission detonated 100 nuclear weapons in the air over those mountains. Later it tested even more in the ground under them.

They do not test there anymore, so why not drop Test from its name? Perhaps Nevada Site would mean nothing, and Nevada Nuclear Site would mean too much. Whatever they call it, the tunnel-ridden site is closer to the highway than the gunnery and bombing range.

All this map-and-sign trivia has put me on notice that I could be zapped, bombed, or neutralized at any time. Or, more realistically, I could run into the descendant of some gold prospector's burro, turned loose hereabouts long before I was born.

Just south of Beatty, the highway makes an abrupt turn. Were I seeing this on the Travel Channel, pretentious music would swell up to reveal the dramatic change of scenery. The brown desert suddenly disappears. Green and tan bulrushes take over. Above, the leaves of spreading cottonwood trees spin in the wind. Squatting low in the bulrushes is a sign, the hand-painted silhouette of a frog. It reads Frog Crossing. I like Beatty already.

The mountains that earlier were away from the highway, now rise 1,500 feet beside it, creating an instant, inviting rock-rimmed hollow. It soon becomes as pleasant a green valley as exists anywhere in this otherwise arid state.

Fresh water from an underground river founded this town. Two nearby mining camps, which later became significant towns—albeit short-lived—had a shortage of drinking water. For a time, water from Beatty was hauled to the miners in whiskey barrels. There was no shortage of those.

I made a slow "windshield" tour of town. Spread over a square mile, Beatty's 1,900 residents live in mobile homes, essentially. It's easy to buy a lot here and order a house delivered. Wood is very expensive in a state that is mostly sand, which may explain the lack of frame houses here.

The Powder Horn, a gun shop, was closed. I got out to read the bronze plaque in front. It read: "On This Spot in 1897, Nothing Happened." Clever, but not as original as the frog-crossing sign.

Beatty's three hotel-casinos, one at each end of town and one in the middle, survive on travelers who drop in off U.S. 95, visitors from central California and Death Valley tourists.

At the north end of town, I pulled into the Rio Rancho RV Park. Cottonwood fluff swirls on the ground. Between shade trees in front, half circling a fire pit, enough wood was neatly stacked to relieve the chill of many evenings. Each RV site had a redwood picnic bench. Each site also had sand-filled coffee cans, painted white and stenciled BUTT. Cigarette smoking is still big in Nevada, unlike neighboring California, where it is almost against the law.

The main building sits back from the road. Its front is a long, covered porch with chairs. A half-dozen people, all Norman Rockwell characters, appeared comfortable and very satisfied there, watching people like me stir up the cottonwood fluff.

Ray Stevens, the manager, left his chair to greet me. "And we also have free wine and coffee," Ray added, "from seven in the morning to seven at night."

"Seven in the morning? Wine?"

"Sure, welcome to Nevada!"

I plugged in the motorhome and joined the Rockwell group. Within an hour I had met almost everyone in the park and had learned about the town from Skinny Forsyth. He has lived here since 1961, but not in the RV park. He comes by every day to visit.

Looking for videos, ice, snacks, or maybe some wine, most of the overnight visitors eventually come by the porch. They quickly get caught up in the sit-and-visit lifestyle that permeates this place. Life at Rio Ranch—for some here, life itself—focuses on the porch. Within a day, I was part of it, too.

The post office is next to the park. Much of Beatty parades by the porch to pick up mail during the day. After a couple of days, I began to recognize those who walked or rode a bike. As for those who drove, someone else on the porch usually knew the car.

Take the late-model sedan that Fran drives. "There goes Fran," someone would always say. According to Skinny, "When anyone in town needs help, Fran is always Johnny-on-the-spot." She owns Fran's Ranch, the local brothel, just outside town.

Among the hard-core porch people was Bill Bridgeman from Arizona. After walking his four dogs, Bill's day begins here with Ray's coffee at 7:00 and ends here at dark. In between, when his wife Liz watches the soaps, Bill usually visits a casino and invests in the nickel slots. Bill wears tattoos from his years in the Navy and bib overalls from those as a Missouri rancher. Now, at age seventy-one, he is interested in old cemeteries. He wanted to show me one.

So we took off in his pickup. On our way to the ruins of Rhyolite, we passed huge, multicolored piles of crushed rock from a mine called the Bullfrog. The flags of Canada and the United States flew over the mine offices. Bill said that the flags of both Canada and Australia are common fixtures at the mines in this state.

I asked him why.

"I had the same question when I first came here," Bill said. "Mining companies are international in scope. They go where the minerals are. Obviously, what they want they find here in Nevada."

Rhyolite was the fourth-largest city in Nevada in 1907, with 6,000 residents. Fifty freight cars a day arrived here on the Las Vegas & Tonopah Railroad, and more on two other lines.

The elaborate railroad station in Rhylolite, much of which still stands, was the finest in Nevada in 1908. It still is in my book. It is a gorgeous and classic piece of Old-West architecture. To identify it with an earlier era, an esoteric art form, or as a European architectural style might be academically correct. But to me, wars have been fought for lesser causes. It is as unpretentious and all-American as cowboy boots or Bill's bib overalls.

The roofless stone shells of a few three-story buildings outline Rhyolite's main street. Once they had stairs of Italian marble, windows of stained glass, and wood trim of Honduras mahogany. Their sun-bleached walls, now stripped by scavengers and weather, have crumbed some but remain today, as do six residents. But Rhyolite as a town is a ghost.

Bill turned the truck onto a narrow cut in the desert and stopped at a fenced cemetery. Mounds of sand and rock remain the only visible signs of the hundreds buried here. Wooden markers lay by a few graves, but most had long since released their epitaphs to the wind.

Bill pointed to one clearly marked grave in the corner. It was that of "Panamint Annie," buried in 1979. Panamint is the name of a mountain range rimming Death Valley, but who was Annie? We could only guess. Perhaps it is enough to know that she is here and forever has a claim to a piece of the desert guarded by the Panamint Range.

13

Old Saloons and Tiffany Lamps

Goldfield, Nevada

The Sante Fe Saloon rests on a dusty side road that may well have been main street at one time. Over the last century, the heavy boots of miners have scuffed out hollows in the wood floor of the saloon deep enough to hold spilled beer. Although it seems more than one saloon in Nevada claims title as the state's oldest, about this one in Goldfield they get specific: "in continuous use." It was built in 1905, but its bar of dark mahogany is even older. It came around Cape Horn by ship and was hauled to Goldfield from San Francisco on a wagon train.

A sign taped to the ornate bar advertises cactus juice at $1.50. "That's for the people on the tour buses from Japan and Washington and the like," the bartender said. Placing a beer in front of me, he asked, "You driving through, or what?"

"Little of both. I want to see what's in Goldfield."

"Then you're about seventy years too late," insisted a man hunched over an empty glass one stool over. "We had here the biggest city in Nevada once. It had trains and fancy dressers and the famous stage show, The Zigfield Follies, one time. Now you could put the whole town up for a night in the Goldfield Hotel and the building would still be half-empty."

"Hell, Jack, the hotel's been closed for fifty years. There's no way. No beds in there, even. You ain't gonna put nobody up there for the night," came advice that was a little slushy and slurred from further down the bar.

"I know that. I was just making a figure of speech." The man shook his head, rolled his eyes, and turned to tell me about the hotel.

The four-story Goldfield Hotel, when it was built in 1907, was said to be the most modern, elegant, and elaborate hotel west of the Mississippi. It had the first electric elevator. Each room had a phone. Many rooms had a private bath with both hot and cold running water. The floors in the lobby and restaurant are composed of hand-laid mosaic tiles. The ceiling of the bar and dining room, which held 400 people, are covered with twenty-two-karat gold leaf. Wyatt Earp dealt cards in the casino after he retired. And Theodore Roosevelt slept there. Attempts to renovate it have gone bankrupt. It stands empty today, as it has since 1945.

Unlike many mining towns in Nevada that sprouted overnight, Goldfield was well planned, surveyed, and mapped. Its population topped at 20,000 plus around 1913. Mines here produced $2 million in gold, and that's when it sold for $16 to $20 an ounce. This still stands, apparently, as a record take, and is believed to be unequaled by any other gold camp in the world.

It's ironic that Nevada's one-time largest city is now the seat of the state's smallest county. Esmeralda County has 1,410 people. The courthouse, built in 1907, buzzes with county business and is as "downtown" as Goldfield gets. The recorder's office, where ladies still labor over table-size ledger books, has concrete walls almost two feet thick. Iron curtains still roll down over the windows, like louvered garage doors, every afternoon at 4:55.

Inside the courthouse I admired the fifty or so cattle brands, burned on patches of cowhide, that cover a first-floor

wall. "Upstairs is the courtroom. I have the key if you want
in," whispered a small voice from the stairs.

"Sure would." I followed Sarah Ridgeway into an immacu-
late, grand sanctuary of Old-West law. She is the courthouse
housekeeper, although she calls herself the custodian. Being
so petite, the title of custodian may describe her job, but it
does not describe Sarah.

Elegant Tiffany lamps adorned the front corners of the
judge's bench. Their stained-glass shades were a brilliant red
and gold. The window blinds of unfinished oak, exposed to
the desert sun more days than most men live, hung straight
and true. Sarah ran her fingers over the manufacturer's
plaque, tacked to the bottom blind. "Look, they were made
in Burlington, Vermont."

On the wall, above the judge's chair, is the head of a
huge bighorn sheep. Sarah explained that the hunter who
killed it took only the head and left the carcass for the
scavengers. That's against the law. The hunter pleaded guilty
in this courtroom. Others, some from as far as Las Vegas,
were willing to pay the hunter's fine and buy the mounted
trophy. The judge instead decided it would stay in Esmeralda
County. What better place than his courtroom? "So there it
hangs," she said proudly.

Sarah pointed to the wall fixtures. "We don't use those
carbide lights anymore. And the ceiling fans finally played
out, so they put in air-conditioning." She squinted and lowered her voice to a near whisper. "But it detracts a little bit, I
think."

Obviously, Sarah felt possessive of the courtroom and its
legacy. And well she should. For the last twenty-five years,
she has polished the brass boot rail in the jury box, dusted
the feather-grained woodwork, and lovingly cleaned each
piece of stained glass on the Tiffany lamp shades. This magnificent courtroom appears to be as much her home as where
she lives.

The new computer by the witness chair Sarah called an
eye-sore. "I hate to even dust it," she remarked.

Early-day cattle rustlers were taken from this courtroom often to face a hangman's noose. "But they still go on trial here," Sarah said, sending me downstairs to get the details from her friend the sheriff.

"We haven't hung one for some time," Sheriff Ed Penson joked, "but we convicted one here two months ago."

With only seven deputies and 3,700 square miles of country, Sheriff Penson admitted rustlers are hard to catch. But this time he got lucky. "I was searching for this guy on the Lida Ranch. If you don't know it, it's a local spread bigger than the whole state of Rhode Island. It even extends into California. After chasing him in his truck through some pretty rugged country, I finally got him. He was turning loose six unbranded calves."

Cattle rustling in this day is not peculiar to Nevada, but what Goldfield's justice of the peace told me certainly is. Pulling on her judicial robes over her sweatshirt and jeans, she recounted the story.

It seems that when she was a court clerk, a man came to her to file a suit in small claims court against the Cottontail Ranch, a well-known brothel south of town.

"He claimed he didn't get his money's worth," she said with a smirk.

"Who won?"

"Oh, I talked him out of it, told him he needed a witness."

"And that ended it?"

"No, he thought about it for the longest time. I thought for a minute that he was going to come up with one. Then he took his hat and walked out. Never seen him since."

Back on the road, I could just imagine what the TV tabloids from the big city would do in Goldfield with a case like that. I'll bet Sarah wouldn't let them in her courtroom and the sheriff would back her up.

14

A Class Act of the Old West

Tonopah, Nevada

The steep approach to Tonopah on Highway 95 cuts my speed so that the forty-five miles per hour speed limit was purely academic. Hills rising on both sides of the road are heavily scarred from years of mining. To call Tonopah a century-old mining town doesn't distinguish it from others in Nevada, except from those founded on free drinks and all-you-can-eat buffets. Its population is 2,500 and dropping.

The mines here produced $150 million, mostly in silver, between 1900 and 1950. The town peaked in 1906 with sixty saloons and a railroad that ran until 1946. Its population shot from 3,000 in 1902 to 10,000 in 1906. Four years later, it was 3,000 again.

The Army Air Corps built a base just outside town during World War II. It was given to the county in 1947. The Air Force became a significant employer here in the 1950s and kept Tonopah whole after the mines closed. Now, the Air Force has all but pulled out.

Today the town hangs on with the help of county government (it's the seat of Nye County), a small mining operation, a struggling tourist business, and boundless optimism.

The owner of an overstocked pawnshop on Main Street told me, "We have been up and down before. The mines will kick in again, or the Air Force will create some good-paying jobs here. I'll wait it out. Got no choice."

The Station House, at the south edge of town, is Tonopah's biggest private employer, with 105 employees. Although the all-night sign in front reads Station House Hotel and Gaming Saloon, it is also a mall where you can rent videos, get your teeth fixed, or apply for state welfare. Behind the casino, there is a bare strip of asphalt with nineteen RV hookups, which has only its convenience to the casino to recommend it.

When I met Station House manager Oliver Crickmon, he was having breakfast—a bowl of cold cereal—at his desk. A shaded window, his desk lamp, and the glow of five black-and-white TV monitors dimly lit his office. The monitors showed the front desk and the dining room and seemed to switch around the casino with close-up and overhead shots of the three blackjack tables.

He explained that Tonopah's labor force now is mostly in the service industry, which pays the minimum wage and little more. "Tough to build a growing economy on that," Oliver said.

A second casino is in the center of town in Tonopah's finest building, the Mizpah Hotel. This magnificent, five-story classic—a true historic landmark—was built in 1907. It has been sensibly refurbished to preserve the best of the Old West, as good as the good life got back then. Most of the rooms still have toilets that flush with the pull of a chain and iron bathtubs that stand on clawed feet.

Jack Dempsey was a bouncer and bartender in the hotel, when he wasn't working in the mines. Wyatt Earp stayed here often. He owned the Northern Bar in Tonopah. His brother Virgil was a deputy sheriff in neighboring Esmeralda County. And Howard Hughes got married here, but several other places can make that claim, too.

The Jack Dempsey Dining Room is heavy with rich mahogany. Brocade silk covers the walls. Its raised design is deep red and feels like velvet. The doors have beautifully etched, inlaid glass. A person who knows might properly call this Victorian style. I claimed it for John Wayne, ladies in ruffled dresses, and the Old West.

Bill Allison, age sixty-six, has owned the Mispah for thirteen years. He calls the hotel the "grand old lady" and runs her as she begs to be run: with good taste, twenty-four-hour attention, and the unrealistic love of a dreamer. Although its rooms are full most all the time, the Mispah has seen better days, economically. "Too many mistakes in the past," Bill says philosophically, realizing that his dream may die because of them.

The closing of the old hotel would be especially tragic. It's the class act in town. Without it, Tonopah has none.

Still, things have a way of bouncing back in this town that silver built. Bill may lose his dream or "give it away," as he puts it. If so, someone will surely come along and pick up where Bill leaves off. Whatever keeps these Nevada towns alive, it may yet save the Mispah.

15

A One-Sidewalk, One-Airplane Town

Mina, Nevada

Eugene Gates keeps his airplane, a two-seater Cessna, tied down next to his house between his big satellite dish and the monitoring station of the National Weather Service. To take off, he taxies for fifteen minutes. He steers his airplane down Helda Drive, crosses Wedge Street, takes care not to brush the trees by the Boyd's house, angles off on a road graded from the desert, and finally reaches the airstrip.

Gene has been a pilot for forty years and an amateur-radio operator for fifty. At age seventy-three, he has three jobs. The most recent one he began twenty-four years ago. Obviously, when Gene starts something, he keeps at it. Probably the only thing he ever started with the intent of stopping is life here in Mina. When he and his wife came to Mina in 1954, they planned to stay just a year.

His twenty-four-year job, with what we used to call the Weather Bureau, does not pay anything. "They set up the equipment. All I do is read the numbers every day and keep a log."

Gene opened a mineral assay office in Mina almost the same day he got here. Whether it's delivered by courier from a mining company or dragged in by a dirt-poor prospector, if it's a mineral, Gene tells them what it is and what it's worth. That's what an assayer does. Gene's success is not because he is the only one between here and Reno, it's because he is the best. Samples for analysis come to him from all over this hemisphere, and some from Africa.

During the last three years, mining has slacked off dramatically in this mineral-and-gem-rich state. New federal laws have turned mining, even prospecting, into a bureaucratic nightmare. "Environmentalists have really made it hard for the little guy, who is out there digging on a hunch, and very expensive for the big guy," Gene insisted.

Gene is also a judge. He is the longest continuous-sitting judge in the state. He has held the elected office for thirty-one years.

"Nobody runs against him anymore," Ruth Fanning told me. She has lived here fifty-one years and ought to know. I met Ruth on the sidewalk. Mina has just one sidewalk. It runs a ways along the west side of Front Street. Front Street is also U.S. Highway 95. I came in on it yesterday.

Ruth and her teenage granddaughter Kim were trying to see through the dirt-streaked windows of the Burger Hut. Although they pass it on their walk every day, this day they were curious. "It's been closed for a year, but the lady who ran it is back in town. We hope that she will open again. Good cook, that lady," Kim said.

I walked with them for the remainder of the sidewalk. We passed a building with fiberboard sides and a sign: For Sale: Two Lots and a Shop. "You could buy a new Ford in there, when I came," Ruth remembered.

"Over there, the train used to stop every day." Ruth's hand, gripping a can of Diet Coke, swept the horizon across the street. "All that was depot and freight office and all imaginable kind of railroad stuff."

The splintered remains of a railroad station and a transfer warehouse were all that remained. It once belonged to the Nevada & California Railway, a division of the Southern Pacific. From the sidewalk, the station looked like a collapsed house of Pick-up Sticks that no one may touch until someone has counted the score.

"It's been that way for nine months. The guy they paid to pull it down...well, he took off with the payroll." Ruth stopped walking. "You know, I wonder why somebody hasn't hauled off that wood and built something."

The railroad founded the town in 1905 and named it for the daughter of a railroad executive. Mina grew with the railroad and the mining industry, but it was never a boom-town like some in Nevada.

Most of the tracks had three rails to accommodate both the standard and narrow-gauge trains.

The narrow-gauge train, the local shuttle, was called Slim Princess. Indians were allowed to climb on top of the cars and ride free. The paying passengers and crew often shot jackrabbits, ducks, and sage grouse from the windows of the train. It would slow so that the shooters could run out and retrieve whatever they shot. On hot days, the train always arrived late. How late depended on how long the crew stopped at the swimming hole.

Today, the railroad is gone. Even the tracks have been pulled up. With the bungled demise of the railroad station, little of Mina's heritage still stands. What remains rests in the finite memories of old-time residents like Ruth.

"This was all bars and barber shops, but it burned." Ruth was referring to a block of weeds and desert grass along the sidewalk. An old hotel appeared on the verge of falling over. Its brick walls were leaning at precarious angles that would tempt a Vegas oddsmaker. Heavy plywood nailed over its windows may be all that keeps the old hotel standing upright.

It's too early in the day for the Mina Club to be open. It's a bar that advertises free coffee for truckers. Just outside town is a brothel called Billie's Day and Night. It, too, advertises free coffee, but for anybody.

Kim told me that someone wants to open a brothel right in town. Ruth couldn't believe it. "It's true! It's on the agenda for the town meeting Thursday night!" Kim insisted.

So we stopped in Jackson's Mini-Mart to read the agenda for the town meeting. Ruth's daughter Theora Jackson always posts the agenda and whatever else people want posted there. Sure enough, next to Margaret's three-by-five card advertising free cocker spaniels was the one-page agenda. Under "New Business" was the following: "Linda Levier's request for citizen support for establishment of Happy Harry's Whore House in downtown Mina."

I talked later with Phyllis Perry. She works for the judge. "It's not a real whorehouse. From a crafts class up in Luning, somebody knows this Linda lady. She's from Hawthorne, in her forties. Her husband is a teacher. She wants to make it a tourist attraction, sell souvenirs. Claims it would put Mina on the map."

"Sounds crazy!"

Phyllis nodded. "Sure, but they'll get a pretty good turnout Thursday night."

Mina's sidewalk runs out before Sue's Motel. Sue's is not a place where a guest would likely find little bottles of pink shampoo and conditioner in the bathroom. But I bet for a couple of quarters, the bed will vibrate you to sleep.

There is nothing but sand between Sue's motel rooms and the road. There, eight guys were strapping on motorcycle gear and having a good time at it. They were on a tour, exploring Nevada's mountain country by motorcycle—old mining camps, ghost towns, the remote places where few people go. Each day for them ends in a different town.

The leader and organizer of the tour, Matt Ernst from Reno, provides the Suzuki off-road motorcycles and the truck and driver to haul their baggage from town to town. Matt said that he has strict requirements about who goes on these wilderness excursions. "The crazies who want to tear things up don't make it. I don't want them. I have to go there again, remember." Nor will he take anybody from Nevada or neighboring California, saying, "You wouldn't show the locals your favorite fishing hole."

These guys roll in here periodically on Matt's Suzukis. They come from all over the country, spend a night here at

Sue's Motel, and maybe have dinner at the Silver King Café across the road. The next day they are at it again, exploring Nevada's abandoned outback. They will probably never come back or even remember the name of this town, but their encounter with Nevada will stick with them. Nevada has a way of doing that.

16

Potluck Booze Made Pizen Switch

Yerington, Nevada

Pizen Switch. What a great name for a town! That's what it was, and would still be, were it not for some persnickety latecomers who didn't much care for its derivation. Pizen, with a long i, was what the miners and cowboys called the homemade whiskey that sold for ten cents a cup at the Willow Switch. Known simply as the "Switch," it was a dirt-floor saloon with a roof of bulrushes and a siding of willow switches.

The potent pizen made at the Switch was potluck booze that never tasted the same twice. When the pizen barrel got low, most any liquid was considered a filler. Peddlers of hair tonic, liniments, and turpentine could often unload a whole wagon at the Switch if their timing was right.

As things typically happened in the Old West, the saloon and everything around it became known as Pizen Switch. Road signs pointed to it. It was a scheduled stop for the stagecoach.

Then the new-fashioned reformers, who today would first have to parade their cause on TV talk shows, created a ruckus by arbitrarily renaming the town Greenfield. That was in 1873. After that, you could tell the old-timer from the newcomer by which name he called the town.

This grudge lasted until the townspeople were overcome by universal greed, which they called "a quest for growth." The railroad was coming west. They all wanted to be part of it. The general manager of the railroad was named Yerington. To butter him up, they gave the town his name in 1894. It didn't work. The railroad went elsewhere. All they got was a rail spur, and Nevada got a town named Yerington.

Today, with a population of 2,400, Yerington is on Alt. U.S. 95. An alternate highway is normally a short offshoot that parallels the main road. This alternate, however, is 106 miles long, goes through three towns, and even twists a bit. A whole new highway number might make navigation more intuitive through here, less complicated. I guess if I am going to roam the back roads, I will just suffer the complications that go with it.

For many, probably most, the cultural and social centers of this farming and ranching town are Dini's Casino and Casino West. The owners of both are blood relatives and descendants of Italian ranchers who, along with many Portuguese, settled this rich valley.

Dini's is the oldest family-owned casino in the state. Known for good drinks and the best food in town, its customers are essentially local and mostly retired. The casino floor is an overcrowded maze of glowing coin machines, mostly nickel, that play every game of chance but craps. Dini's has one blackjack table, but the game is seldom played for lack of a dealer.

Almost next door is Bryan Masini's Casino West. It's bigger, less down-home than Dini's, but again, its patrons all seem to know each other. Bryan, in his forties, a father of four and an active member of the school board, became a state-licensed casino operator at the age of twenty-four—the youngest yet.

The tidal wave of family-fun centers now flooding Las Vegas has trickled into Yerington. Obviously, a casino's sole existence is to promote its games. If it takes a carnival ride for the kids to get their folks in the casino, the kids will get their carnival ride.

The Masini casino/motel complex now has a movie theater, a swimming pool, a twelve-lane bowling alley, a mini-mart, a video-game room, and an RV park. To call it an RV park, really, is stretching it. It's a parking lot with utility hookups behind the casino. But I stayed there a couple of days. I thought it might get noisy and maybe wild at night, but it never did.

The keno game at Casino West has aged well, considering its hardware may have been built by the game's inventor: two spindles, a hole punch, a lighted display board, and a spinning wire barrel that blows out numbered Ping-Pong balls.

Take off his red tie, white tennis shoes, and jelly-donut-size belt buckle that read Casino West in sterling, Sal Pezzino could be an orchestra leader or college professor. He's got that look of intellect. While most proper keno games operate with a minimum of three people—manager, writer, and runner—Sal is a one-man show. On his feet most of his four-to-midnight shift, he never takes a break. His dinner is delivered when a waitress gets to it. He runs to and from the men's room. Facing Sal's corner dominion were a row of empty chairs and a table. Even with no apparent players, he kept running games as if all Nevada were watching. "I've got multi-race tickets," he explained. "You can play up to five games ahead." Sal is seventy-three and a widower.

A lady all in pink, including hair and eyeglass frames, gave Sal a flirtatious greeting and filled out a chair. One hand, heavy with yard-sale jewelry, was black as coal from rubbing money. Sal appeared to have neither the time nor the interest to give her much attention. She played no keno and soon left.

At the table, a lady about thirty-five in a glittering Uncle-Sam outfit called herself Sage Saber. "That's my professional name. Do you want my real name?" she asked me.

"No, one's enough."

Sage explained that she is a psychic, astrologer, and numerologist. She also conducts seminars on Eastern medicine and holistic health. Today, she was here running a bazaar.

Sage is hard to miss in her tall, sparkling gold hat rimmed with a red, white, and blue banner. I ran into her later seated in front of a slot machine. She was losing big time. For you or me, it would simply be bad luck. For a fortune-teller with her credentials, it must be have been calamitous.

A side-street building, which over the last century has been everything from the city morgue to a poodle parlor, is now the Hitchrack Deli. A burned-out Merrill Lynch broker from Boston, Joe Arnote, runs it. He came here in 1987 because Nevada is the cheapest place in America to open a bar.

"Small towns are great. When I opened this place, even my competitors sent me flowers," Joe said, as he pulled out a sheet of aluminum foil to wrap a "to go" sandwich. "I can tell you right now," he stopped to look at his watch, "who is in Dini's, what they are drinking, how many they have had, where they are sitting, and probably what they have on." Joe laughed. "What's that tell ya about a small town?"

"Habits die hard, I guess."

He handed the sandwich to a waiting customer.

"Small-town people." He paused. "They accept you for what you are. What you once were doesn't matter. There is no pretending or fake stuff in this arena. A phony won't last six months here. This town is too tight a circle."

Joe said that many come to his place from the casinos after they have lost their twenty bucks for the day. "This has become a gamblers' refuge. I don't see them much when they win. So I see them a lot."

I spent my last night in the hills above Yerington at a new but almost empty RV park overlooking the old Anaconda copper mine at Weed Heights. Anaconda left behind an open pit 650 feet deep and huge piles of dirt. An Arizona company is now processing that dirt, shipping out 40,000 pounds of pure copper a day.

In the row of RV sites behind me, an old and rust-streaked Coupe de Ville cranked like a new one but did not start. Even from here, I could smell the gas. I walked up to the couple inside and offered my guess: "It's flooded."

The man got out in a rage. Through white hair that covered his face like a string mop, I could see his red eyes, wide with anger. He slammed the driver's door and kicked it. I was afraid that I would be next.

"I know exactly what's wrong! Total obliteration of dynamism. Absolute. Total."

"That's it, for sure. It's nice that you know about cars," I said, backing off.

"Aliens have controlled this planet for ages. They turn energy off and on, on and off." His arms moved up and down like pump handles, synchronized with the rapid wrinkling and unwrinkling of his brow. "I have an appointment right now. That's the reason. They don't want me to get there. So the car will not start. No dynamism! It's that simple! Later, you watch, it will start in a snap."

"I'm sure it will. You guys have a nice day, now." I took a few more steps back.

He pulled the hair away from his face. "I've seen what they do. Can't see them, because they are on a different visual frequency than us. You should know, I mean you really should, they have no use for us men, but they inhabit women's bodies. My last three wives, they tore 'em up." He turned away. "Got to go now!"

He and his lady friend walked to a pickup truck. It cranked. It started. Off they went.

"Oh, good, that truck has dynamism," I muttered, not too sure that someone, somewhere, wasn't listening.

Part II

Northern California — Oregon

17

Isolated by Its Hugeness

Mount Shasta, Northern California

The conical peaks of the Cascade Range run single file from northern California toward the Canadian border, where Mount Baker pops up in Washington like a bookend. Mounts Shasta, Hood, Adams, St. Helens, and Rainier are the preeminent snow-covered pressure valves for the most volcanically active range in the continental United States.

Headed north on U.S. 97 in California, I decided to pull off the road and have lunch where I found a clear view of Mount Shasta. Fortunately, a thoughtful road builder had found just the spot and had built a wide shoulder there to park on. I stepped from my motorhome, staring at a mountain so enormous it filled the landscape. It took some staring just to take it all in.

Dining in the grand presence of Mount Shasta, it seemed inappropriate somehow to be serving myself an unadorned ham sandwich with a glass of nonfat milk. I spread on a layer of Grey Poupon. That helped.

Haloed by a wisp of cloud that streamed off northward, Mount Shasta is isolated by its hugeness. That it towers to 14,162 feet seems less significant than the hundreds of square miles over which it spreads its soft yet jagged vestment of stark white. It dominates everything, even the sky.

A few miles back, I walked the main street of Mount Shasta City. At 3,561 feet, it rests at the foot of the mountain. Mount Shasta's peak, however, is a deceptive ten miles away and two miles up. It's an orderly town of trendy shops, four-wheel drive vehicles, and comfortable mountain homes. Most have a healthy pile of firewood neatly stacked outside. And the ladies who shop there, even those in jeans and ski jackets, wear expensive perfume.

18

California's "Highest" Town

Dorris, California

U.S. 97 originates in Weed, California, about twenty miles from the Oregon border. After running through the mid-sections of Oregon and Washington, it becomes the Alaska Highway in the middle of British Columbia and merges into Highway 1 when it enters the Yukon.

Its last town in California is Dorris. Traffic slows to fifteen miles per hour here. Not only is it the speed limit, the road also makes four ninety-degree turns. Since I was going so slowly anyway, I stopped in Dorris.

A sign put up by the Lions Club solicited donations to erect America's tallest flagpole. I wondered if they know about Calipatria, another California town that right now boasts America's tallest flagpole at 182 feet.

"Yes, we know about it, but not much. It's down by San Diego someplace, isn't it?" Donna Burcher, the city clerk, handed me a brochure about the Dorris flagpole and a donation envelope. "Our flagpole will be 200 feet high. We think it will give a positive impression on people coming into the state here. You know we are the highest town in California, so that's another reason."

I challenged her claim to the "highest town."

A man at a desk behind her spoke up. "She means the highest like on the top of the map—in latitude, not elevation."

"That's what I said. We are the highest, the furthest town north."

Back in the motorhome, I ventured even higher, into Oregon. The next town was Klamath Falls, population 18,200. Tied to lumbering since its infancy, Klamath Falls was once the primary supplier of packing crates for fruit farmers. That all ended in the depression years of the 1930s. And from my view of the town from the highway, not much has happened here since.

The highway and the tracks of the Southern Pacific Railroad skirt the edge of Upper Klamath Lake north of town. (Lower Klamath Lake lies in California.) It's the largest natural lake in the state, but very shallow. Today its gray, choppy surface appears about to splash out icicles. A cloud bank that could bring rain, even snow, obscures much of the other side.

Although snow-covered ridges rise from the edge of the lake, the highway is at lake level, maybe even below it in some spots. It may be an optical illusion, but it appears that the bed of the railroad serves as a levee, keeping the lake off the road. Were it not there, things might be pretty wet where I am. It is too cold out there to stop and check it out, so I will never know for sure.

19

It's Illegal Not to Have a Gun

Chiloquin, Oregon

Pulling off the highway to skim the surface of the little town of Chiloquin, I crossed the railroad tracks. Westbound Amtrak trains come through here on the way to Seattle.

In the late 1800s, trains of Pullman cars stopped here, full of anxious fishermen. The Pullmans were parked on a siding for a week while passengers fished the Williamson and other rivers. This was all Indian country then. In fact, Chiloquin claims to be the first town incorporated on an Indian reservation. That happened in 1926.

A sign on the door of city hall said Closed, but the door was not locked. John Hall, head of public works, and Lillian Headly, city recorder, were wrapping up their day yet seemed inclined to share a little of it with a stranger.

John told me that he never takes the keys out of his car. "Nobody steals things here. We all have guns. It's a city ordinance."

"What? Never heard of such a thing."

"That's right! It's the law. If you are going to live in Chiloquin, you are going to have a gun."

Lillian reached into a drawer of her desk and pulled out a two-page copy of the ordinance dated June 14, 1982. Sure enough, "every head of household . . . is required to maintain a firearm, together with ammunition therefor." The only ones exempt are those too disabled to use a gun, those whose religion prohibits it, and convicted felons.

"I suppose what's important is that the word gets around that Chiloquin is an armed camp," I said.

John grinned, "I don't think of this town as any 'armed camp', but if the bad guys want to think that, that's OK."

I stopped for the night at the Waterwheel Campground, which is right on the river. Ray Poteet and his dog Maddie met me at the door of the log home that he and his wife Kerry built in 1991. They live upstairs. Downstairs is the campground office and recreation room.

That Ray and Kerry should run a campground—they have always spent most of their free time in an RV—is the realization of a dream at its finest. Now in their mid-30s, both had good jobs in the San Francisco area. They gave all that up in 1989 to live life on their terms in the outback of southern Oregon.

Their log house, surrounded by wooded hills, seems a perfect fit for the Poteets. Made of machine-turned lodge-pole pine, it is obviously Ray's pride and joy. A woodstove heats their 1,800-square-foot house. "The logs act like storage batteries, picking up the heat when I have the stove going," Ray explained. "Then they radiate it the rest of the time. Once the logs get cold, it takes a few days to charge them up again."

That night it snowed. Ray warned me that it would dip into the twenties by dawn, so I drained my water hose.

As soon as there was light, I stepped outside into the fresh snow. With each step, the frozen grass crunched with a sound like breaking glass. It was so loud, I feared it would wake my neighbors. Just a dusting of snow, but it was everywhere. Steam rising from the river transformed the frozen air into something lacy and ethereal.

I call this the "fairy-tale feature" of my nomadic life. A new view from the window every morning. An early morning walk in a place where I have never been. I love it out here. I really do.

Overhead was a wild, clamorous sound that cut even the chill. High in the April darkness flew skeins of snow geese, honking northward in undulating V-formations across the dark sky. Necks stretched toward Canada, their white bellies cast an eerie glow as if reflecting the white of the new snow. Absolute trust in their instinct, it pulled them north into a new season.

20

Where Flies Come to Die

Prineville, Oregon

Walking around the parking lot behind the Crook County Courthouse, I tried to line up a picture.

"What're ya looking at?" came a voice from the driver's window of a little gray pickup.

"I want to get a picture of the clock tower, but the sun isn't right."

"How long ya going to be here?"

"Not long enough for the sun to be on the front."

"Sun's never on the front. Ya wanta go up in the tower?"

I didn't know why I should see the tower from the inside. Obviously, this experience was to be had by invitation only.

"Sure," I replied.

"Come on back around three-thirty."

He sped away. I gave up on the picture.

My first day here and I was already on the good side of Fred Farrish, the maintenance man for the most important and tallest building in Crook County's biggest and most important city: Prineville, population 6,000.

Killing time until three-thirty, I picked up a copy of last week's Central Oregonian. A section called the "Law Enforcement Log" reported a sixteen-year-old male cited for "minor-in-possession of tobacco." I read it again. It said exactly that.

That intrigued me enough to look up Russ Miller, the managing editor of the newspaper. Russ was in his office. "The experts call tobacco a 'gateway drug.' They say it precedes drug and alcohol use," Russ explained. "So the town has an active campaign to cite kids when they catch them with it, which is often. It isn't just cigarettes. Chewing tobacco is a bigger problem because it's a 'cowboy thing.' Kids see a lot of that being used around here." Russ went on to say that the people of Prineville have the largest percentage of church affiliation of any city in Oregon—something like 80 percent.

The north edge of town is where the nineteen miles of Prineville's railway start. It's proof that the gutsy pioneers of the American West were still running things here in the early 1900s. It seems that they could not persuade the mainline railroad to come to them. So they built their own railroad to the mainline.

It was a cattle town then. Farmers and ranchers from a hundred miles around came here for their supplies and entertainment. All Prineville needed to secure its future was a railroad. So in 1916, the town voted 358 to 1 to build it for an estimated $100,000. Despite volunteer labor and food and wagons provided free by farmers, the cost of construction tripled. Still, they got it done. Freight and passenger service was running by 1918.

Then came the motorcar and the Great Depression. Had it been privately owned, the railroad probably would have gone under. But the town continued to back it, confident that someday sawmills would be built here to tap the area's timber, one of the largest stands of ponderosa pine in the country.

They were right. The rail line became very successful. So successful that Prineville was called "The City of No City Taxes." Railroad profits paid for everything governmental, including a new city hall. The line still operates every day, makes jobs for people here, and makes money for the town.

It is the oldest municipally owned and operated rail system in the country.

Jerry Price is the general manager of the railroad now.

"On weekends we operate dinner trains that can be mystery-theater or maybe western-hoedown trains. Sunday mornings we have a champagne-brunch train. During the week, we haul freight, timber products almost exclusively. Outbound, it's all wood chips that move to mainline paper mills."

"Wood chips?"

"Ya, like what's left after you cut trees into boards."

"But I thought trees here are like endangered species and cutting them is prohibited."

"You are partially right."

Then I got a course in the facts of life and real-world economics in the lumber business. It seems that the sawmills in this Oregon town—in America's vast Northwest with millions of acres of standing timber—are importing trees from faraway Mexico, Chile, New Zealand, wherever they can be bought. It's not that foreign timber is cheaper than trees cut locally. That would be easy enough to understand. It's that special interest groups in our country, protecting owls and other things, have been able to prohibit tree cutting in vast areas of the Northwest. Instead, as Jerry put it, "The sawmills do what they have to do to stay in business."

At the corner of Third and Main Street is Prineville's rotating-time-and-temperature building, the Bank of the Cascades. Across from it is Bank Drug, which once was a bank. And across from it is the Bowman Museum, which was once two banks. First it was the Prineville Bank, later the Bank of Prineville, or vice versa. No one was too sure.

Behind the counter of the Bowman Museum, I found one of those important and dedicated ladies to whom we back-road dawdlers are indebted. What would the museums of small-town America do without them, these unselfish volunteers who open thousands of museums for us every day? They all seem to share deep feelings for their heritage and an out-and-out disgust for daytime TV. Built in 1910, the interior of this building is like new. The teller cages are marble and mahogany, the windows faced with thin bars of bronze. When I was told that it's made of the same black/gray basalt as the courthouse, I looked at my watch. It was 3:20.

Fred was waiting for me. We rode the elevator to the third floor of the courthouse.

"When there is a jury trial going on, I don't even come up here to wind the clock. Too many people. It will run six days. I wind it on Mondays and Fridays," Fred told me.

I followed him up some steep wooden stairs to the attic, which had a floor of rock-wool insulation. Filling one of the eight windows was a rain-stained piece of plywood. "Window got blown out by the wind," Fred said. He seemed in no hurry to replace it.

More steep stairs. I used the handrail.

The next level had floor-to-ceiling windows that were open to the wind and framed with ornate iron bars.

"Someone told me the jail was up here," I remarked. "Now I know why people would say that."

"Ya, people think it. Even still, some believe it. If they would come up here and look, they would know better. But people believe what they want to believe. How do ya change that?" The higher we climbed in the tower, the wiser and more philosophical Fred became.

We climbed the last flight of stairs. "This is where flies come to die, because it's warm," Fred observed. "In the summer when I sweep, I can get a whole bucketful."

It appeared to me more like a giant fly trap, but Fred knows best.

This was the top. A three-story clock tower atop a three-story courthouse. The clock ticked away on a platform in the center of the room. Some rather simple gears turned four shafts that turned the hands on four giant clock faces, the four translucent walls of the room.

In the corner rests a wooden box with "The E. Howard Clock Co., Boston" printed on the side.

"That's what the clock came in," Fred explained. "I suppose it's out of warranty now. Maybe we can throw the box away."

Using both hands, he turned a crank on the clock. Up came a wooden box of dusty rocks through a hole in the floor. "It runs like a cuckoo clock. The rocks are the weight that keeps this town on time.

"When I bring schoolkids up here, some are surprised to see that the clock has four sides. It makes you wonder. They must look at the clock from different places around town, but in their heads, they think of it as having just one face. Makes you wonder, doesn't it? Does me!"

21

The Driftwood Capital

Bandon, Oregon

There are more trees than anything else in Oregon. Since they line the state's 350-mile coastline, it is no surprise that some end up in the ocean. But why do so many pile up on the beaches near Bandon? So many, in fact, they have made this little coastal town the driftwood capital of Oregon, perhaps the world.

Driven by furious winter storms, the logs pile up beyond the high-water line. This is not casual driftwood of which lamps and clock faces are made, but gigantic timbers and stumps measuring ten feet in diameter and weighing tons. These are the tailings of lumbering operations in the mountains east of here, along with those nature has cast into the Coquille River, which empties into the ocean at Bandon. I am told that there is a lot of exotic wood in there too: mahogany, yew, teak, redwood, and bamboo. Driftwood collectors here won't guess—and don't want to know—where it comes from. They say the beauty of driftwood lies in the mystery of its origin: "Nobody knows from where or whence it came."

Tossed by enormous energy, the timber collects in colossal, haphazard heaps. Giant trees balance crosswise on the rock jetties that form Bandon's small-boat harbor. Tourists on scavenger hunts rummage through the piles, looking for something to take home. Local kids dig and crawl, routing out secret hideaways. They gather on summer afternoons to eat peanut-butter sandwiches deep in the twisted timbers.

To be driftwood, a sun-bleached, gnarled log is not enough. It must first wash ashore. This qualifying process can be spectacular, even terrifying.

From miles around, in their rubber boots and yellow slickers, the dedicated come to watch. They have formed a group called the "Storm Watchers."

Ruth Ball is one. "Gale winds at high tide make for some awesome weather," Ruth said. "The water has such force and power, yet it's so grand and graceful. It gently lifts huge logs and then drops them, sends them rolling and crashing all over the place. Oh, we have beautiful storms."

Bandon wants to be called Bandon-by-the-Sea. Why they cite the obvious and put a tourist spin on a perfectly fine Irish name is, unfortunately, what people do now. The economic focus of the coastal towns of Oregon is U.S. 101. It runs through all of them like a feeder tube. Forming a two-lane edge of the state from top to bottom, it flows with tourist dollars from Washington and points north. Even more dollars flow from the south, particularly from southern California.

Although locals love the dollars from southern California, they would do well to tolerate those who bring them.

"I don't know what happens to people down around LA. I think they teach arrogance in the public schools," an out-of-work logger told me as he pulled in smelt, two and three at a time, off a dock in the boat basin. "I guess when you see the world every day through blackened windshields and barred windows, it warps ya, like watching too much news. They come here on vacation and complain because their cellular phones don't work. I'd be glad, if I were them, on vacation and all."

The drizzle blowing in from the ocean now became heavy. The logger offered me some smelt as I turned to leave. "Take some. Ten of these make a good meal."

"Thanks, but I'm going to treat myself and eat out tonight."

Getting wet didn't seem to bother him. He continued to pull in fish as I dashed for my dry motorhome.

With "reservations recommended," Harp's Restaurant has the feel and soft music of a shirt-and-tie place. But owner Michael Harpster, a transplant from Riverside, California, greets guests in jeans and shirttail. Tonight, he is maitre d', busboy, and wine steward. The success of Michael's fine, dinner-only restaurant tells something of the sophistication of Bandon-by-the-Sea. It also says that a few more bucks come into this coastal community than meets the eye.

That night, the wind came in over the Coast Range and blew the sky so clean it looked distilled.

At Ballards Beach State Park, I walked from my motorhome to where sandpipers ran at the ocean's edge, poking their bills in the sand after every wave. With the sun just coming up, the blue Pacific shot silver all the way to the horizon.

The nearby lighthouse competes with Face Rock, on the other side of town, as the most photographed landmark in Bandon. One or the other usually adorns the cover of the local telephone book. Built in 1896, its light went out in 1939 when it was hit by a ship—a distinction hard to come by for a lighthouse.

A young couple hunting agates were the only others this morning on this long, beautiful expanse of sand. I remembered the logger's words about another place: "where you have to take a number to get on the beach." The couple tent-camped in the park last night. Yesterday they found a large glass ball being tossed about in the surf. Coveted by beachcombers as an artifact from a foreign land, it had gotten loose from a fishing net. Japanese fishermen, operating in deep waters off the coast, use them as floats on their tuna nets. When the tide went out, the couple searched for sand dollars. They claimed these creatures collected gold for ballast.

I too started a search: for a newspaper, a place to read it, and a cup of coffee. It was easy to find the Coos Bay World, but I had to ask to find Lloyd's.

Some call Lloyd's a typical logger's café. Coffee is ready by six, as are hot biscuits, which are made fresh every hour. It's in Old-Town Bandon, surrounded by shops rigged out in macramé, perfumed candles, stained-glass mobiles, and Snoopy beach towels. Two arches over the street label Old-Town Bandon with Welcome on one side and Come Again on the other. They appear as facades to the synthetic world of tourism. But Bandon is not a synthetic place. Neither is Lloyd's.

I sat at Lloyd's counter midst a local longshoreman, a cranberry grower, a retired postal worker, a sheep rancher, and a man who rents crabbing rings to tourists. The Coos Bay World, however, was superfluous.

Item: Foreign fishermen are vacuuming the ocean off the Oregon coast while "our guys sit here." They can't compete. "We have in this country the highest standard of living in the world. For shame, we refuse to pay the wages to support it."

Item: In 1949, Bandon had one policeman and a Ford pickup truck. He shared the truck with the mayor, who used it to read utility meters. One Saturday night a lumberjack, "drunker than a boiled owl," angered the cop. The policeman went to draw his Colt 44, which he had never done before. But it went off before he got it out of the holster and he shot his toe. The lumberjack, somehow, hauled the cop off in the truck to get his toe fixed.

Item: Logging has been banned in much of the Northwest since May 1991. Meanwhile, 7,000 U.S. loggers are unemployed. Bureaucrats and environmentalists balance national priorities: the survival of America's lumber industry against the possible loss of an owl species. "Whatever happens, the economics of the industry are now skewed forever."

Item: Settled by Scandinavians and Germans, the immigrants now coming to Coos Bay are from California. They make up about 40 percent of the town's population.

Item: A sales tax in Oregon? "Never happen!"

Item: This is Tuesday, one of two days a week when the Bandon Cheese Factory hangs out its Curds Today sign. Curds are just-made cheese, fresh from the tub. True curd connoisseurs get them before they have chilled.

At 10:15, I was at the Bandon Cheese Factory. A cart of fresh curds rolled out from behind the glass window that separates the room where they make the cheese from the room where they sell it. A salesgirl wrapped her hands in plastic and bagged the still-warm curds.

Chewy and delicious, curds squeak when you chew them. Hence their nickname: squeakies.

A group of us stood around eating our squeakies like popcorn, right from the bag, as we watched the girl bag more of the pale-yellow chunks. She told us that when the curds age for a couple of days, they lose their squeak. Aged for a few months, the curds become cheddar cheese. Aged for a few years, they become sharp cheddar, which sells for six dollars a pound.

"Now, why is a man like cheese?" she asked us.

We all stopped eating.

"Like cheese?" someone stammered. "Is this a riddle?"

I ate another squeaky, thinking it might give me a clue.

"Give up? They both begin soft and warm, eventually lose their squeak, and with age become sharper and worth more."

I'd like to think so.

22

This Trucker Hauls His Two-Year-Old

Oregon 140, Eastbound

Only every third vehicle was a car or a pickup. The rest were logging trucks. Those coming at me were loaded, headed for Medford. The others carried the back wheels of the trailers piggyback, atop the rear wheels of the tractors. The shafts that connected the two telescoped. They extended over the cabs like artillery pieces.

Mt. McLoughlin, its 9,495-foot cone resting on the tops of the trees ahead, shimmered with a massive snowpack. Winter storms, just past, had ended a seven-year drought in the Northwest. The snow line was low for early June. The biting contrast of ice-white against a cloudless sky caused distance to fall away. I knew I was about to feel the chill of the mountain, the remnants of winter.

It didn't happen. Nature had suckered me again. It turned out Mt. McLoughlin was thirty miles away, deep in the Rogue River National Forest. After a few more miles, I never saw it again.

The scent of cattle and wildflowers fills the air along Oregon 140 where it begins in western Oregon. Leaving Interstate 5, it climbs the southern Cascades on broad shoulders into timber country. A yellow snow zone sign offered a clue to what a winter driver might expect. One with six bullet holes offered another clue.

Still climbing, my side windows were even with the tops of tall fir trees. Down was a long way. The guardrail looked as if it might stop a small car, but it would do little more than tell a search party where to look if I hit it.

After an hour of climbing, my carburetor was sucking thin air. I pulled into a spacious parking area beside a flooded alpine meadow. A Peterbilt truck with a long load of Boise Cascade trestles was there too. Bill Hastings & Son, Wolf Creek, Oregon, was lettered in script on the door of the cab.

Never on the road, on a CB radio, or in person have I encountered an unfriendly long-haul trucker in my travels. I trust them. If nothing else, we have the road and the weather in common. Most truckers work alone. Some travel with their wives or girlfriends. Bill, in the Peterbilt, was the first I had met who traveled with a two-year-old.

Putting aside his logbook, Bill swung open the door of the cab. Jessy James Hastings crawled into his dad's lap, dropping most of his baloney sandwich between the seats.

"I have custody, so he pretty much goes where I go." Obviously, Bill liked it that way. "We run from Medford to Salt Lake a couple of times a week."

Bill climbed down to my level and reached up to the seat to retrieve Jessie. "He's a great traveler. But there are times!" He addressed Jessie. "It's tough to sleep with little fingers prying your eyes open."

Like most over-the-road trucks, Bill's Peterbilt has a bed behind the seats. Some truckers have TVs, stereos, and VCRs back there.

Bill knew the area well. "Elevation here is 5,100 feet. We are on the Winnemucca-to-the-Sea Highway." (Winnemucca is in northwest Nevada.) Oregon 140 doesn't really go all the way to the ocean, but another road does. On winter week-ends, snowmobilers and cross-country skiers pack this parking lot.

I figured Bill would know why logging trucks are collapsible.

"For a good reason. At the loading dock, back in the woods, there is not a lot of room for a big rig to turn around. So they get the truck pointed out, put the back dolly on the ground, reassemble the reach, and load it up."

I left Bill to finish his logbook entries and started on the downside of the Cascades. Soon his red Peterbilt filled my side mirror. We chatted on channel 17 and coordinated a place for him to pass.

A big truck is amazingly quiet when it overtakes you. The roll of eighteen wheels makes a low, well-machined purr. Mixed with the wind, it's a sound of the open road, a reassuring hum heard nowhere else.

The highway rolled out of the mountains and into a meadow. There, the waters of Wocus Bay lapped at the edge of the blacktop. Upper Klamath Lake again. I had come full circle. Though I could see only half of it, the lake was deserted, just as before.

This was a revealing statement about Oregon that figures only hint at. Nearly 97,000 square miles. Only 2.8 million people. Most of them are 300 miles away, circling Portland. Nature's battle in this millennium may be with man's ignorance and greed. But there are so few of us around here, nature seems at least to be holding its own.

Parts of Klamath Falls are tiered on a hillside. The industrial part, which shows clear signs of the lumber industry starving to death, surrounds Lake Ewauna, more a river than a lake. Under certain sections of the town are boiling springs, which form a stratum of hot water. Piped through radiators and grids, the water heats homes and offices and melts snow from sidewalks.

I pulled into a commercial campground for the night. This one seemed more carnival than campground. I tagged along behind a "follow-me" vehicle to my numbered campsite. Did they think I would get lost or maybe run down a kid racing to the video games? I am not accustomed to this. Maybe it is a nice touch, though. What next? A chocolate on my pillow?

23

Harley-Davidson vs. Honda

Klamath Falls, Oregon

The new-day sun, filtered by the leaves of old cedar trees, settled first on the grassy tent area of the campground. Minutes from their flannel wrappings, two men sat there like stone figures. Their eyes were fixed on the hypnotic sparkle of three chrome-loaded Harley-Davidsons and a Honda. A third man stood behind them, slowly peeling a banana.

Another fellow walked into the frame of this otherwise still life. He was doing well with his hands full of topless Styrofoam cups that appeared to be overflowing with coffee. He had no place to set them, so he just stood there waiting for a couple more hands. The banana-peeler went to his aid. The coffee was passed around. A conversation began.

Twenty years in the planning, this was the trip of their lives. They were just three days into it. Two were teachers in the California prison system. Two others were from Hawaii, one a cowboy and one a musician. They were motoring through the back roads of California, Oregon, Washington, and British Columbia.

Harley owner Barry Bongberg carried a cellular phone, just in case someone needed to reach them. "We forget to turn it on when we said we would," confessed Barry. "At least, that's our story when we get home."

Their coffee was gone in no time, so I had walked over with a fresh pot. We sat around and let the sun start to warm things.

"I know there is some grand mystique." I was searching for the right words. "Really, what is it about a Harley?"

"Oh! The sound! The vibration! But mostly the rumble. Bet you didn't know that 'Harley Davidson' is the most popular tattoo in America."

"I would have guessed a girlfriend's name, or maybe 'mother.' "

As a worker in a men's prison, Barry is probably the best-qualified authority on tattoos that I will ever meet.

"No, 'mother' went out long ago," Barry explained. "Then there are those that guys got in Vietnam. Really bizarre, like daggers and snakes and some military insignias. But 'Harley' is still big."

The fellow who brought the coffee said that the Harley is really the only motorcycle made. Everything else is a toy. He was baiting his buddy who owned the Honda.

The Honda owner was not to be put down. He addressed me exclusively. "Did you know that Harley Davidson is really a T-shirt and belt-buckle company? It's true. Their bikes are just a merchandising gimmick that they ship in here from Mexico."

We finished the coffee and kidded around for half an hour. Then they suited up, loaded their gear, and rumbled off.

Out here on the road is the only place you will find guys like these. Barry and each of his companions have happy lives where they work and live, but I bet they are not the same people there. People change out here. They take on a freer spirit. Or maybe it's just how they look at things. Life becomes simpler. Laughter comes easier. Yesterdays are quickly forgotten because they don't matter.

24

A White-Circle Town

Bly, Oregon

Back on Oregon 140, I turned east. KWFA, "your nostalgia station," was playing "Near You." A sign read five miles to Olene.

Olene is nothing more than a general store, like thousands of America's mini-towns, those tiny, white circles on road maps. Each store evolves into what the locals want from it. But the stores have one thing in common these days: they all rent videos.

Quite often in America's backcountry, there is no broadcast TV at all. Many homes now have satellite dishes. But for everyone else, videotapes are the primary source of entertainment. Like TV itself, they have become a what-did-we-do-before necessity.

Another road sign, this one understated: "Abrupt Edge." This highway, which yesterday had paved shoulders wide enough to camp on, was now a slender, precarious piece of aerial roadway running hills and grassy chasms with bravado.

I stopped at Bly, another white-circle town, in front of a district office of the U.S. Forest Service. Painters blocked the visitor's door. Directed to another one, I instantly found myself in the office of two chatty civil servants, who apparently had little happening today but were full of news.

With timber sales on public land almost down to zero, the Forest Service is now in the mushroom business. Their new enterprise sprouted earlier this spring because of last year's Robinson Spring Fire, they told me. Mushrooms thrive the first year or so in areas swept by forest fires. Although the public may harvest two gallons of morel mushrooms per person free on the north side of the highway, the Forest Service is banking money from commercial mushroomers who work the south side.

"The Indians can pick all the mushrooms they want," one lady said, "but they must be for subsistence only. That is, they must eat, not sell them."

The other lady corrected her. "Native Americans, you mean."

"I keep forgetting. Old ways die hard. I can't keep track of it all." She laughed. "Whatever is politically correct is what we go by."

"You know, the Indians came here from someplace else, too," I said, "just like my ancestors."

"Tell that to my boss."

25

Living Close to the Land

Lakeview, Oregon

The people in Lakeview have not had a lake to view for the better part of a century. No one especially cares. It's been so long, nobody remembers when Goose Lake covered nearly a quarter-million acres and lapped the southern edge of this Oregon town.

But they had reason to care last summer. The lake disappeared completely, and its talcum-dry bottom blew into town on the wind. It was one gray-dust storm after another. The storms made the air so dense, the town disappeared more than once. Pulverized alkali settled everywhere. Even brewed coffee took on a strange flavor, they say.

After a drought-busting winter in the Northwest, Goose Lake is back, but nowhere near where the town's Irish settlers found it in 1876. And it probably never will be. It's been shrinking, some years more than others, since it last overflowed in 1890. It fluctuates so drastically, Lake County statistic-keepers will only talk numbers in terms of averages. It's a big lake, usually thirty miles long and ten miles wide. Give or take a few, its shoreline averages eighty-two miles. It covers 124,000 acres, with 65 percent of them in California. Now, this figure explains why Goose Lake ebbs and flows like a tidepool: it doesn't go deeper than eight feet. With water spread that shallow, it does not have to lose much to shrink the shoreline. When it's low, people walk or wade across it, just to say they did.

As the crow flies east, Lakeview (population 2,600) is the last town in southern Oregon. Between it and the Idaho line is 200 miles of high desert and low mountains.

A hundred miles west is Klamath Falls, where most things come from. The Red Ball Stage Line round-trips a van there twice a day, hauling newspapers, mail, passengers, and whatever. Not just its name, its mere existence is reminiscent of an Old-West stagecoach and underscores what people here say they like most about Lakeview: "We're isolated, nobody bothers us, and we do what we damn please."

Scattered in front of Don's Market is horse tack, hay-rake seats, a couple of sleds, a holster for an M-1 rifle, and other rusty antiques usually found hanging or maybe buried in old barns. They are John Bach's display. John has more inside.

For a couple of years, John made a living (enough for a bachelor) selling groceries here on the edge of Lakeview. That business dried up when the Safeway in town became a round-the-clock operation. So he diversified. Mixed in now with racks of Wheat Thins and Frito-Lay cheese dip are his "collectibles": rocks, bottles, bells, clocks, a wind-up train, and the like.

I spy a table made of lamp-oil boxes. "Classic. Depression: primitive style," said John.

I sat on a high stool. Duct tape holds the vinyl seat cover in place. Half-listening to Rush Limbaugh on the radio, I watched John. At the counter, he unwrapped a towel from a Civil-War bayonet. A customer, as close to the countertop as a 300-pounder could get, bowed at the waist to have a closer look at it.

They both turned to greet someone. It was the postman. "I know who gets this before I see the address," he said, handing John a gun catalog. Then he stepped to the cooler, pulled out a pint of milk and a container of potato salad, dragged a stool around, sat down, and ate lunch.

John, age forty-six, was born in Lakeview. So was everyone else who came in the store that hour. Like Ike Wells, the sergeant with the six-man Lakeview Police Department. He was one of John's classmates.

Ike buoyantly recounted the highlights of yesterday. "Four miles over scab-rock flat, down a slippery cow path a mile. And would you believe, somebody had been there first? It ruined our day, until we caught a dinner's-worth of rainbows. Along with fresh-picked mushrooms and stuff, we fried 'em up within spittin' distance of the creek."

John turned to me. "It's our passion. Fishing and hunting is what we do up here." He shook his index finger. "Except for one lady," he laughed and pulled on the visor of his Ducks Unlimited cap. "She was from California, and I hope to God she still is. Chewed me out royally for being a hunter. Came up to watch deer, she said. I asked her, 'Did ya see any?' She said 'Yes.' I told her, 'You can thank me for that.' Ohhh! That really unscrewed her. I told her that the hunting-and-fishing license fees I pay go for wildlife management and conservation. And still, deer starve to death here every winter. If you are looking for a shame, that's a shame, I told her."

John began sorting through his mail. A small box with a hand-lettered address required a pocketknife to open it. It contained three strings of Indian beads.

"You know," he looked out the door and pulled on his cap visor again, "we are fiercely independent up here. Comes from living close to the land." John ran the beads through his fingers. "We are not afraid of much, but if we fear anything, it's people like that. They are great at imposing their ideology, their values, on other people. They pull that crap around here, there will be a problem, I'll tell ya."

I looked at Ike, the cop. Ike gave a nodding endorsement.

The big city has its men's club with its two-martini lunches and its power dinners. Lakeview has Don's Market, an old-time general store without a potbellied stove, like Cheers without a bar.

At 4,900 feet, Lakeview calls itself "the tallest town in Oregon." Although most of the state's lumber industry spreads along its western side where the trees grow faster, Lakeview has two sawmills. It had more. But this is mostly ranch country now. Sheep were in this valley first. Now it's mostly cattle. During the summer, Lakeview County's 83,000 square miles have many more cows than people. In October, most of them are trucked south to snow-free pastures in California.

A couple of ranchers, Chuck and Treva Kelly, decided years back to share their 8,000-acre cattle ranch with RVers. Their Junipers Reservoir RV Resort, on Oregon 140 ten miles west of town, is centered in what is as much a wildlife refuge as a ranch. It is spectacular in its openness and natural beauty. I drove in for one night and stayed seven.

Camped in the tent area nearby were two hang glider pilots from Berkeley, California. Lakeview is popular with hang gliders. The area has good thermals and some high, straight-down places from which to jump, which hang gliders call "foot launching."

Bradley Ream, a commercial photographer when not clipped to his gull-wing airfoil of aluminum and Dacron, invited me to come along and watch. We drove up a dirt road to a point 2,000 feet above town. While they assembled their gliders, a weather radio in the car repeated information about wind velocity, temperatures, and the like. Bradley has over 3,000 hours in the air, nine of them on one flight.

"The glider is not as flimsy as it looks," he said. "In fact, it can take more Gs than a 747." Bradley pulled on his flight suit, strapped on a parachute, and then zipped his upper half into what looked like a mummy-type sleeping bag. Once in the air, he would pull in his legs, wrapping himself up completely.

Bradley said they would fly until they ran out of thermals, their source of lift, probably an hour or two. He expected to land eight or ten miles up the valley. They had hired a local high-school boy as their chase-car driver.

In the air, Bradley carried with him a small oxygen bottle, an altimeter, a two-way radio, and a book. The radio was to direct the chase car to their landing site. The book was to read until the car got there.

Strapped to his wing, Bradley ran across the road and silently drifted off the edge. Hanging under the canopy, he swept out a couple of figure eights. Going higher, he caught a good thermal, just what he had come here to find.

Riding back to the Junipers in Bradley's chase car, we drove by Don's Market. Ike's police car was parked in front. So was a mail truck. It was noon.

26

The Sucker Jar of Surprise Valley

Cedarville, California

Eleven candy jars crowd the counter at the Cedarville Grocery. Some open at the top, but the one holding the flat suckers opened on the side. A little hand reached up but couldn't quite get the cover off. So I lent a hand. Out poured the suckers: red, green, orange, transparent, all individually wrapped in slippery cellophane to make them slide out easier. The little hand got what it wanted. I spent my first few minutes in Cedarville repacking a sucker jar.

"Why do you stuff it so full?"

"We have to buy in big quantities," came the reply from someone seated behind three colors of sour twist. "It's all trucked in, you know."

"No, I don't know. So you crammed the whole truckload in here, is that it?" I tipped the jar on its side, figuring if no one else helped, gravity would.

"That's the trick. Now screw the top on."

"But it will just happen again to the next guy." I was trying to be helpful.

"No, it won't. People here know how to do it."

Dave Hunt came from behind the counter with a handful of gardening gloves. He slid them on a rod protruding next to the fishing bobbers, under the shelf of shaving cream.

This is Surprise Valley, in the northeast corner of California. I was at its crossroads, its only four-way stop.

My morning began in Oregon but soon changed to California somewhere along Highway 395. Before the town of Alturus, a sign pointed to Surprise Valley. The name attracted me, so I took the road eastward toward it. It was a long climb over Cedar Pass, elevation 6,345 feet. On the way down, I decided that I would find another way out. Tomorrow.

Tomorrow, like four others, had come and gone. I am still in Cedarville, population 800. This town, this whole valley, could not be farther from a big city if it were on the moon. It has a solid foundation of self-sufficiency and independence that shows on people's faces, the way they talk and conduct business. I love it here.

Cedarville is the largest of four towns, all tied to one road fifty-four miles long that runs the length of the valley. To the north, the road ends at Fort Bidwell, which was the last outpost of the U.S. Cavalry. Continuing southeast, it becomes Nevada 447 and goes on to Reno, 200 miles away. The only other road out that is not gravel is the one over Cedar Pass.

Along the eastern side of this narrow valley lie three shallow lakes heavy with alkali. If they were freshwater lakes, this valley would be a resort. During drought years, as most of them have been recently, the lakes dry up and become alkali flats. Good for nothing when wet, they are a playground for wind surfers when dry. The rest of the valley is either hay fields or grazing ground for cattle.

Surrounded by mountains, their peaks pocketed with snow well into the summer, this valley is remote. Its very existence was obviously a surprise to those who named it. Some would call it isolated, which it certainly was once, but no place is truly isolated anymore in this country.

Still, the valley's 1,500 people are definitely removed, even divorced, from the state in which they live. Many prefer it that way. The newspaper, delivered here daily, comes from

Klamath Falls, Oregon. California's Sacramento Bee is on sale at the drugstore in Cedarville, but few people seem interested enough to buy it. (Sunday's Bee was still in the rack on Wednesday.) Television is all cable. Curiously, the system carries not one California station. Local TV-news shows seen here originate in Medford, Klamath Falls, Reno, and Chicago. AM radio is almost nonexistent, except for one Klamath Falls station. People here think nothing of driving 150 miles to shop in Klamath Falls. With no sales tax in Oregon, most prefer it to Reno, another option. No one I found expressed allegiance to California.

In fact, some businessmen, Ed Hunt in particular, would give anything to see the state line moved west fifteen miles, putting them in Nevada. "I spend half my days working for the bureaucrats in Sacramento," Ed says.

Hometown pride focuses on the whole valley. The letters cut in the mountain over Cedarville are not C but SV. As for state identity, people here feel a kinship more for Nevada or Oregon than California.

In between weighing hay trucks at the public scales, Harold Asherman told me, "Voting in local elections is the worst. We are so cut off from California, we never know who is running or what they're about." Harold and his wife Ruby came here in 1966 to run the general store in Fort Bidwell. They are now retired, but the store remains one of the longest continuously operating general stores in California.

Rod McQuillan teaches math in the valley schools. In the early 1970s, he and his wife Jackie left southern California bound for Idaho. But they found Surprise Valley first and never left. In 1989, they bought the fourteen-room Sunrise Motel and RV Park in Cedarville.

"He's made of spring steel," someone said of fifty-four-year-old Rod. Followed everywhere by Ralph, his foot-high terrier, Rod starts his days at 6:00 a.m., unless the sun comes up earlier. Like most small-town entrepreneurs, Rod has no fantasies of getting rich. In fact, he is taking out most of his revenue-producing RV sites to put in trees, shuffleboard, and a putting green.

"Why create amenities for motel guests who just come here to sleep?" I ask.

"Makes my head feel good."

Janet Irene is another high-energy entrepreneur who understands small-town economics. A few years back, she stood in front of her half-empty duplex on Main Street and wondered, "What should I do with this wonderful old building?" Now alone, her two children grown, the valley has been her home for twenty-five years. "Maybe a place for folks to eat," she thought. Although her only experience with restaurants was having eaten in a few, she drained her savings and turned half of the duplex into the Country Hearth Bakery and Restaurant. As money came in, she expanded it. "I don't believe in borrowing," she said. "People should not spend what they don't have." Fact is, she doesn't even take credit cards.

"Surround yourself with what you like and make your work your hobby," is Jan's approach to life. As for surroundings, her needlepoint decorates the restaurant. Kerosene lamps with tall glass chimneys dress every table. At night, they light the restaurant. "In Georgia, where I grew up in the Okefenokee Swamp, the glow of a kerosene lantern adds a soft sweetness to everything."

Boarded-up buildings tell of what worked here once but doesn't anymore. A movie theater. A flour mill. A trading post. All castoffs. On some buildings, For Sale signs tell of abstract hopes. On others, caved-in roofs tell of no hope at all.

Without a doubt, the American pioneer still flourishes out here. Their covered wagons go faster, their roads are better, they have most of the comforts and discomforts we all share, but they live close to the land. While our predecessors of a century ago made towns from almost nothing, these pioneers are reshaping them from what was left over and left behind.

Most buildings in Surprise Valley have been recycled and reclaimed, many more than once, but never replaced. Some have simply evolved. For example, the combination pool hall, bar, and paperback library in Eagleville—the next town over—was built in 1891 to be a general store. Which it was and might still be were it not for the guy who somehow hauled a pool table into the valley over Fandango Pass. That was in 1931, the same year he put the pool table in the store. Today, the original plank floor of the old store has a boot-worn furrow circling the pool table. Obviously, the folks in Eagleville wanted a pool hall more than they wanted a store. Apparently, they still do. The store was never renovated. It just evolved.

Dave Hunt's corner grocery, built in 1900, is a recycled branch of the Bank of America. He's got the vault to prove the building's ancestry. He just wishes he had the vault door.

"And now you take in cash for vodka and chewing to-bacco," I said, examining his behind-the-counter inventory. I had stopped to say good-bye to Dave on my way out of town.

"We sell a lot of chewin' tobacco." Dave leaned his chair back on two legs and reached for a can of mint snuff. "You know what this is? It's snuff with decaffeinated tobacco. . . de, denicotined is what I mean. I can always tell when it's time for the road crews to get their annual physicals. About two weeks before, they start buying this stuff." He held up the can. "Don't know who they're fooling. Somebody, I guess."

I told Dave that I was heading south but would be back someday.

"Don't open any sucker jars!"

27

The Oldest Living Things

The Sierra Nevada Mountains

The Sierra Nevadas thrust their jagged peaks far beyond the timberline, the forest habitat of the largest and the oldest living things on Earth. A single block of granite, the Sierras form a continuous barrier along much of the California-Nevada border. Stretching about 400 miles, they run half the length of California. Winter in these mountains allows southern Californians to boast of skiing on fresh snow after breakfast and swimming in the ocean after lunch.

They are the loftiest mountain range in the country (excluding Alaska), with a dozen peaks rising more than 14,000 feet. Forests of pine and fir cover the western slopes to an elevation of 9,000 feet. Here are groves of sequoias, some of the largest trees in the world, and three national parks: Yosemite, Kings Canyon, and Sequoia. At lower elevations grow bristlecone pines, the oldest known living things. The range was named for the Sierra Nevadas in Spain, which contain that country's highest mountains. There the word means "Snowy Range."

It was the Sierra Nevadas, tame and running out of elevation, that I crossed to get into Surprise Valley. Now I travel east of them, heading southbound through Nevada. To get on the other side and into California, the obvious choices are the wide-bodied Interstate 80 through Reno or maybe Highway 50 out of Carson City and by busy Lake Tahoe.

If I use either of those, the easiest routes, I will miss something for sure. Those roads are for traveling, not for journeys. The map shows another route, a black line over the mountains with a number 88. It lay just ahead. Why not?

28

Can't Root for the Hometown Team

Alpine County, California

Nowhere in this whole county is there a high-school football game on a fall Saturday or a basketball game when the snow flies. They don't even have a high school prom up here. In Alpine County, kids don't get to eat a Big Mac, hang out in a 7-Eleven, or go to a movie here. Even if they wanted to, they couldn't see a dentist in this county. Credit geography and blame their forefathers for this happenstance. It goes back to 1854, when they were drawing up county boundaries.

Alpine County has no high schools, theaters, Golden Arches, dentists, 7-Elevens, banks, ATMs, or traffic lights. It's tied together by one road that goes over Ebbetts Pass, elevation 8,730 feet. The pass is closed in the winter, which can be six months. So the county is split in two—economically, politically, and socially. That's why Alpine County has no high schools. After the split, it's just too small.

High in the rustic timber country of the eastern Sierras, it is a speck on the mammoth range that is most of California's east side. It ranks eighth in smallness among California's fifty-eight counties (776 square miles) and first in the least number of people. A county official has rounded off the population at 1,200. Others say that's bogus since a third of them don't live here in the winter.

Markleeville, elevation 5,500 feet and population 165, is on the west side of the pass. It is the county seat. Kids here go to high school in the next county, which is Douglas, in the next state, which is Nevada. In fact, people up here do most things in Nevada. They think of it as "downtown," and speak of it as "down the hill." More than that, they identify with Nevada. Many of them fervently wish that they were part of it and get frustrated that they aren't.

Radio stations heard here are all in Nevada. So the talk shows rehash issues of that state and maybe national ones, but certainly not those of California. Their "local" television is from Reno, even on cable.

As in Surprise Valley, the Sacramento Bee is available, but most everybody in Markleeville reads the Record Courier, the daily paper of nearby Minden, Nevada. "How can I do my shopping without knowing where the sales are?" That's how one lady explained her preference for the Nevada newspaper.

Politically, it's a real mess. Local media blanket them with Nevada politics, but to vote intelligently in their home state, it's a research project. Although Ronald Reagan was governor of California for eight years, Nancy Thornburg, a forty-year resident here, admitted, "I never saw Reagan on television until he ran for president."

Nancy is the historian of the county. The magnificent museum here had been her work, more her passion, since 1964. We drank iced tea together in The Deli. Her visit was shortened by a leg of lamb. One of her three daughters was having a thirty-something birthday dinner. Nancy had to leave to get the roast in the oven.

Before leaving, Nancy told me that Jacob Marklee home-steaded 160 acres here, ran a road through it, set up a toll station, and collected money from the wagon trains that passed through. Sounded to me like he was an uncharitable opportunist, but she said it was a common practice then. Wagon masters willingly paid any man who made a road for them. Apparently one person was not so willing, or at least

not happy, with Marklee. His enterprise ended when someone put an ax in his head. Still his name lives in the town he
founded in 1861.

Silver mines boomed here in the late 1850s. That's why
they had to create the county. They needed a place to file
mining claims. Alpine County's population peaked at 5,000 in
the 1860s, supported by mining, logging, and ranching.

Logging lasted after Mother Nature quit giving out silver
and the mines closed. Eventually logging shut down too, not
because Mother Nature quit making trees but because politicians and environmentalists began running the timber industry. Some ranching goes on, but tourism and county government is what supports Markleeville today.

"This county is about 95 percent government land, all
timber. They own it. They control what happens on it. We
used to share in the revenue from logging, but that's gone,
and most of our tax base with it," Nancy explained. She
paused, as if to collect the right words. "The real problem—
the irony of it—is that Smokey the Bear has done his job too
well. We have overprotected these forests to where we can't
touch them. Unfortunately, we can't protect them from what
they are full of—bugs and rot. That creates a dangerous fire
risk that gets worse all the time."

Nancy compared her life in a tinder-dry national forest to
that on an earthquake fault. Disaster will strike someday. The
only question is when. "We are surrounded by a real fire
threat," she said. "What we need, what we have pleaded for,
is fuel reduction. Some selective clearing and cutting. It is too
explosive now."

The degree of fire danger is determined every day by the
U.S. Forest Service and posted at conspicuous places. Approaching town this morning, the sign I read warned of High
Fire Danger. The next level up is Extreme. Beyond that, there
is no warning, at least on posted signs. Last year they had five
days of extreme fire danger here.

The Deli belongs to Warren and DeAnne Jang. They work
in it all day, part of the night Saturday, and live over the
general store next door. DeAnne's parents own that. They

close in the winter and work in their other deli on the other side of the mountain.

Under a tack on the wall are dollar bills. "One for every year," Warren explained. "The first dollar we make each season, we tack up there. The same customer has provided three out of the five."

At the sandwich center, where DeAnne spends most of her day, the line of orders hanging on clothespins was getting longer. Assorted administrators and adjudicators of Alpine County sat under umbrellas on the front deck. The county offices were closed for lunch.

The courthouse, next to the general store, was built in 1928. It's not the oldest building in town but will be some-day. Made of gray stone, it has that look of immortality, the requisite of a county courthouse in the American West. It is definitely unlike the aged, wood-frame structures that line the rest of Markleeville, about two blocks on both sides of High-way 89.

There are no sidewalks. "It saves the trouble of rolling them up at night," Dean McKinley said, from a seat at the bar of the Cutthroat Saloon. The saloon's major business, accord-ing to Dean? "Lotto tickets! Buyers come up from Nevada. This is the biggest Lotto place in California."

"They told me that at Stateline, down on I-15."

"Well, then, the second biggest."

The Cutthroat Saloon, part of the Alpine Hotel, was moved here board by board from somewhere else in 1886. Many of its original square nails still hold it together. This place, and Mario the owner, are popular with weekend mo-torcyclists. In front of the saloon, a sign reads Harley Parking Only.

Dean looks to be in his forties, lives alone on some wooded acreage, seldom gets a haircut, and seems to suffer little from having no visible means of support. "Next weekend is Mario's birthday," Dean told me. "This town will be all motorcycles. Mario throws a free barbecue, the biggest in the state."

Dean looked at me expectantly. I had nothing to say.

"Yep, the biggest in the state, probably anywhere." Unchallenged, he now felt safe with the claim.

Dean goes south in the winter. "I'm back in the spring, in time to see the arrival of the white license plates. They're like an invading species each summer, driving hither and thither, burning up government gas and polluting the air. They ought to be required to carpool and pick up folks hitching rides," Dean said.

"You talking about the Forest Service?"

"Well, the botanists, archaeologists, geologists, and whatever-else-ists they send up here. Most of them are still wet behind the ears. They are not elected by anyone. They don't even live here. I never see 'em at night, like to talk to. Yet they have more to say on what happens in this county than everybody else put together. Shouldn't be! Just ain't right."

With that, Dean stormed out the door and headed across the street. His drink was still on the bar.

"He'll be back," the bartender said. "He just went to get his mail."

Part III

Central California

29

Perched on the San Andreas Fault

San Juan Bautista, California

The Sierra Nevadas at my back, I crossed the floor of California's great Central Valley, the agri-rich San Joaquin. Ahead was the Pacific Coast and, of course, another range of mountains to cross. That's a given. By definition, to have a valley this big, mountains must rise on each side to make it.

Getting over the low Diablo Range was a breeze compared to the Sierras. Highway 152 made it quick and easy. I climbed past the San Luis Reservoir and coasted into the little town of San Juan Bautista.

Perched on a bluff at the edge of town, the Faultline Restaurant looks out over the San Andreas Fault. There is nothing to see, really, because the fault lies under fields of lettuce. But it's out there. Curious people like me come to look, anyway.

The residents of this quiet town, population 1,650, don't make a big thing of living on the edge. But they could hardly be closer to the earth's most famous fracture, which cuts through western California from top to bottom. Slippage and movement along the 800-mile fault, which extends as deep as ten miles, causes hundreds of earthquakes every year, sometimes as many as two or three a day.

The San Andreas Fault is as much a part of the natural environment here as the weather. In fact, the almanac in the weekly newspaper reports local earthquake activity together with inches of rainfall, temperature highs and lows, and lunar phases.

"Most of them are small, magnitudes around 2, maybe a 4 occasionally. Last week there were fifteen earthquakes in the San Francisco area, which includes us down here in San Juan. Were it not for our sensors, and there's a hundred planted around this county, we would never know they happened." Al Balz is the earthquake expert in San Juan Bautista. A volunteer, he looks after the U.S. Geological Survey's seismograph here but claims the title "expert" comes purely by association.

The seismograph—the only one Al knows of that is accessible to the public—sits on a bluff above the fault. Taped to the inside of its glass case are heliographic traces of some significant quakes from as far away as Japan and Bolivia.

"You mean those were recorded here?"

"You bet." He pointed to the trace of an earthquake in the Sea of Japan. "That was a 7.7 magnitude. You can see it knocked the needle off the paper for three minutes. We didn't feel it, of course."

It's ironic that this minute-by-minute recorder of California's contemporary history, so much a part of life here, rests on the exact spot where much of California's early history originated. It was here in 1797 that Father Fermin Lasuen decided to build the fifteenth in the chain of California missions. Looking out over the valley of spring mustard, he was obviously not aware that he was standing on the edge of a geological wonder which, 109 years later, would destroy much of his mission.

By 1823, Father Lasuen's group had founded twenty-one missions along a 600-mile route from San Diego to Sonoma, just north of San Francisco. At each mission, almost as a ritual, they planted olive trees. El Camino Real, "The King's Highway," connected the missions. The route later served as a major stagecoach and wagon road. Today it closely parallels U.S. 101.

Spain claimed title to California then. The missions, each administered by two priests and six soldiers, were a valiant but vain attempt at colonization. Their growth, significant in the early years, was essentially the work of those who were already here—the Native Americans. So Spanish California was little more than a remote, ill-supplied outpost of European civilization.

Mission San Juan Bautista outgrew its first church within a few years. So, in 1812 it opened the largest of the mission churches, the only one with nine bells. Imprinted in its high-gloss, brown tile floor are the footprints of wild animals. Made about two centuries ago, the tiles were apparently spread out on the ground to dry. Animals roamed across the area at night and must have roamed over the tiles while they were still soft enough to make impressions.

In 1906, an earthquake caused the walls of the church to fall down, along with the nine bells. The church was not completely rebuilt until 1976. Only three of the bells were put back. Apparently, it was religious business as usual during those fifty years, as this mission claims to be one—if not the only one—that has never been without a priest since it opened.

Foreigners—Americans, that is—began to arrive during the 1840s. By then, California belonged to Mexico. Among them was the nine-member Breen family who showed up at the mission penniless and were given shelter. They were members of the luckless Donner Party that reportedly resorted to cannibalism to survive the winter of 1846, stranded high in the Sierra Nevada Mountains. The Breens became an important family in town.

The Breen home is now part of the state historic park, on the bluff with the mission. Its focus is a plaza, a square block of lawn surrounded by a beautifully restored building dating back to 1840.

The town of San Juan Bautista grew and took on its own identity apart from the mission. At one point it had four newspapers and seventeen saloons. Eleven times a day a stagecoach rumbled into town. Its main street has changed little since the building boom of the mid-to- late 1800s. Like their occupants, the function of most every building has changed a few times.

The Abbe Mercantile is the town's first brick building, vintage 1861. Every morning before dawn, it is surrounded by the aroma of baking bread, which makes the San Juan Bakery sign redundant. Its brick oven, fifteen feet deep and almost as wide, produces 350 loaves a day. There is seldom any left at day's end for John House and his family to take home. John, his wife, his son, and two daughters work the twelve-hour-a-day business.

When I met John, he was pulling round loaves out of the hot oven with a wooden paddle. Pouring us some coffee, he and his son took one of the rare breaks they get between six and noon.

"Our sourdough bread is the most popular, I think. Maybe it's because our starter is forty years old," John said.

His son James added that they use 2,000 pounds of bread flour and 500 pounds of sugar a week. Then James confessed to his worst day. "I left out the salt. This is not a forgiving business. You can't fix it. We filled a few garbage cans that day, but it will never happen again, ever."

A customer approached our table and asked James how much sugar was in the Portuguese sweetbread. "Fifteen percent."

"That's another thing. People are now very aware of sugar, salt, and fat. We have to know how much of each is in everything. And believe me, they ask. A few years ago they didn't care, or at least they didn't ask."

The morning I left town, I rose early and stepped outside my motorhome. Roosters and peacocks were making themselves known from half a dozen places around town. A crop duster hums somewhere low and out of sight. The chimes in the Glad Tiding Church told that me that it was 6:00 a.m. I walked to the bluff to check the overnight seismic activity. None.

It was Sunday. The sun shone full on the mission. Those who doubt the reality of a God and heaven would have a tough time explaining this day. The serenity of this place at this moment was overwhelming. I thought about going for my camera, but film would only capture the image, a small part of what I was experiencing.

Automatic sprinklers watering the plaza chattered behind me. Under my feet, the ground was black with the crushed droppings of Father Lasuen's olive trees.

30
Jake's Fish Farm

Joaquin Valley, California

I was headed south on Interstate 5, paralleling the California Aqueduct. This water-delivery system has done as much for this state as its weather. Combining nature's most precious gifts, farmers have made the San Joaquin Valley America's year-round vegetable garden. This was originally a bowl of dust and tumbleweeds. Now crops thrive, people work, and the economy prospers. But pools of water here are as rare as trees.

Just driving through it, the San Joaquin Valley seemed an unlikely spot for a fish farm. A guy named Jake Webb, however, began raising catfish here at an age when most men consider it a project just to get through the day. He is in his eighth decade, having begun his career as a fish farmer about ten years ago.

After leaving the interstate, I pulled off Highway 198 just west of Lemoore, an all-American family town of multi-generation farmers and Navy folks from the nearby naval air station. Earlier I was told, "If you don't live there or know somebody who does, don't bother." And I wasn't going to until I heard about Jake.

I pulled into the fenced-in yard of his son Larry's auto shop. Jake stood out in his bib overalls with blue stripes, which almost matched those of his shirt.

I began by telling Jake that I knew nothing about catfish.

"They are slippery and horny. What else do you want to know?" Jake kept taking off his straw hat and scratching the side of his head, but only when he talked. It must have helped him think. "Tell you what. I'm going out there. You best just come along and see for yourself."

We climbed in his pickup and drove back to where two rows of rectangular ponds had been bulldozed out of a field. Dirt was pushed up in mounds to form dikes between them. The flat tops of the dikes were wide enough—just barely—for Jake's big truck.

"I usually use a golf cart on this. Today I've got to fix it," Jake reminded himself.

Each pond or bed was about sixty feet across and a little longer than a semi. Jake said they were four feet deep. Clogs of dirt fell into the muddy water as we moved along the narrow dike. Looking straight down, I began to understand the advantage of using the golf cart.

I asked Jake how many fish were in each pond.

"Hell, what do you mean how many? I don't know." He glared at me. "I can't see 'em. Can you? And even if I could, how do you count fish in a pool? Try it sometime."

Jake again scratched the side of his head. "I put a bunch in a couple of years ago. I can tell you for sure, something is eating an awful lot of food at $300 a ton."

He stopped the truck beside a cluster of pipes that rose from a corner of the dike. We got out. Jake turned a valve. "The cats in here are three years old and weigh probably five, six, seven pounds. Tomorrow a fellow is going to take out about a ton and haul them to San Francisco."

"You call that harvesting?"

"Don't call it anything. We just run a seine down the pond attached to two pickups and pull the fish out at the end." He started toward the truck. "The guy tells me they sell 15,000 pounds of catfish a week in Chinatown.

"I worry about 'em a lot." We resumed our balancing act along the dike. "If the electricity goes off, the aerating towers quit, and fish can't live long without oxygen. They could also get wiped out overnight by a disease."

We passed an employee of Jake's who was standing waist deep in a pond, fully clothed, probing the muddy bank with both arms. Jake explained that he was picking up eggs, the last of the spawning season, for the hatchery.

"The eggs hatch in two to four days at these temperatures. If the water were colder, like sixty-five to seventy degrees, it would take a week," said Jake. In nature, only about 3 percent of the little fish survive, but in Jake's hatchery and aerated tanks and ponds, he estimates that 25 percent make it to adulthood.

"How did you get into this?"

"Stupidity," he replied, slowly steering the truck around a narrow corner of a fish pond. More mud splashed into the water. I had thoughts of the truck doing the same. "I was going to grow cotton, but it cost too much to get started. It's a risky business, I discovered. Channel catfish are like turkeys. If they can find a way to kill themselves, they will."

I didn't get to ask how he discovered that. We got out at the hatchery. Here a paddle driven by an electric motor simulated nature. Jake explained that the "old Tom" stays with the eggs and fans them with his tail to keep them clean. The gentle wave action simulates the fanning motion. It appeared Jake had thought of everything.

31

A Town That Deserves a Medal

Lemoore, California

I drove into Lemoore looking for an air-conditioned place to eat lunch. My motorhome was much too hot. Before I knew it, I passed through town. So I turned around and stopped at the Vineyard Inn.

Because I was alone, I guess, and maybe looked bored waiting for lunch, the thoughtful waitress brought me a copy of the local weekly, the Lemoore Advance. A front-page story announced the school board's decision on the dress code for elementary students. Henceforth it will be impossible to tell the boys from the girls by what they wear to school here. One exception: no earrings for the boys.

Lunch finished, the waitress served me a gift dessert of hot apple crisp. She said something about it being the last piece. Lemoore was taking on a kindly personality and becoming more than just the hometown for people I don't know. What a difference a waitress makes!

Lemoore has always been a service center for farmers. In 1958, the Navy began building an enormous air station ten miles west of town. This gave Lemoore a population boost in the 1970s and 1980s. Otherwise, not much has changed. The jet base poured dollars and people into the community. Life here was uncomplicated, comfortable, and easy. As schools and churches got larger, bonds grew between the long-time residents and the world-traveled newcomers from the Navy.

With their rural lifestyle in common, each came to depend on the other, as people will do in a small town. Local families visited the base for air shows and open-house barbecues. The Navy people attended PTA meetings in town and became serious competitors in the winter bowling league and summer softball.

Then it happened. It came on so slowly, few were prepared for it. It began to build in the late 1960s, along with the growing number of newspaper stories with the words "based at Lemoore Naval Air Station." This little farming community, sheltered from even big-city problems, was being ravaged by a war in a foreign country—Vietnam. Every aircraft carrier deployed from the West Coast to the waters off Vietnam carried two squadrons of jets with 500 officers and men from the naval air station at Lemoore. Many of their families stayed here, living either in town or in quarters at the air station. More than a hundred young Navy pilots and crewmen with families in Lemoore never came back. Some of those families have stayed here. Others have gone elsewhere to remake their lives.

Another unfortunate group of Navy families grew here in numbers as the war dragged into the 1970s: the wives and children of prisoners of war and those missing in action. These families lived in a never-never-land for years, not knowing when their husbands and dads would come home, if at all. Lemoore was probably home to more Navy POW/MIA families than any other community in the nation, at least any community its size. These families could have moved anywhere they wanted, but they have stayed in Lemoore. What they have needed to survive—support, understanding, and acceptance—they have found here.

This small town of fewer than 5,000 people carried an awesome burden for the whole nation. A nation that did not care. Although the lost and missing were not native sons, it didn't matter. They were neighbors. Living with unending suffering week after week, year after year took its toll. It had to.

I found no monument, no plaque, not even a paragraph in the Lemoore Chamber of Commerce's town history that recognized the anguish this proud town must have endured. Then again, who erects a monument to suffering and pain? Certainly not those who have lived it.

Perhaps it is best forgotten. It was a long time ago.

32

Its Name Preceded It

Coalinga, California

The town of Coalinga was so named because of its association with the coal mines. Like so many others in the West, this town began when the railroad arrived. In the mid-1870s, the Southern Pacific Railroad was frantically laying track westward across the San Joaquin Valley. After Hanford, it was a straight shot to Huron, then northwest over the coastal Diablo Range to Hollister. But by 1877, the railroad had crossed the valley and decided Huron would be the end of the line.

At about the same time, oil seeping from the foothills near here was being collected in gallon cans and sold around the valley by peddlers. The cans of crude, like nuggets of gold, begged the question among prospectors and businessmen alike: Was there more where that came from?

The first well produced ten barrels of oil a day, and that was with the help of a windmill pump. But things picked up. By the late 1880s, oil fever was rising like the wooden derricks that were popping up west of Huron.

As oil production grew, so did the problems of getting it to market. The mule trains they were using could not handle it all. The oilmen begged for a rail line to their wellheads. At best, oil was merely axle grease for the railroad or maybe a substitute for coal oil. The railroad had no interest in either. But that attitude quickly changed when coal was discovered in the oil fields. The railroad understood coal. They used it.

In 1887, the railroad ran an eighteen-mile spur west from Huron to loading points it called Coaling Stations A, B, and C. The coal mines played out quickly. Stations B and C were lost even to history. So the coal train then had only one stop: Coaling Station A, which quickly became Coaling A. And that's how Coalinga got its name—and its railroad.

A few years later, the mines closed. But no one cared. An oil well called the Blue Goose was gushing 1,000 barrels a day. The black-gold rush was on, and with it came Coalinga's identity.

From two-dozen frame buildings and some tents and shanties in 1900, Coalinga erupted into a wild frontier boom-town. The thirteen saloons of Whiskey Row stretched for a block. With a reputation for raising nothing but "hell and jackrabbits," Coalinga drew its share of ruffians.

Helen Cowman was ten years old the night that Whiskey Row burned. "Oh, do I remember that night! My father was really upset. The saloons were where everything happened in town. Whiskey Row was like the Yellow Pages. It was where you got your business done."

The oil towns of California were never as wild and law-less as the earlier gold-mining camps. One reason was that the oil companies provided homes for their workers' families.

As recently as 1972, every kitchen sink in Coalinga had three faucets: hot, cold, and drinking water. In the early years, trucks hauled the drinking water from Armona, forty miles away, and delivered it to tanks at each house. In 1959, the front-yard tanks disappeared when the city built one big one and laced the town with new plumbing for drinking water.

"Coalinga water was so high in salts, we were told not to drink it," Audry Acebebo told me. "Some claimed it worked on you like a laxative. Molly Hughes drank a glass every day before breakfast. Said it helped her. Guess it didn't hurt. She lived into her high eighties. We couldn't wash our hair in it because the soap got gummy. It took a rinse of vinegar or lemon juice to get it out."

Audry, curator of the R.C. Baker Memorial Museum, sat at her desk. She poked through shoe boxes of colored stones as we talked. "If you go back to the Indian days, oil bubbled out of the ground as tar. They lined baskets with it, traded it, used it as glue for arrowheads, and even chewed it. There are some caves near here that have an inch of soot baked on the ceilings, so I guess they burned it, too."

She ran her fingers through the stones in a second box. "Going way back, this country was all under water. So we have great fossil beds around. We have a conglomerate here in the museum—a rock, really—that is solid seashells. Takes two men to lift it."

Pointing at the shoe boxes, I asked Audry if she was into rocks.

She laughed. "If you're a curator, you're into everything. These were a gift. You know the expression about someone else's treasure?"

Although the emphasis is on old tools of the oil industry, just being old earns an artifact a spot in this museum. There is a license-plate collection from 1928 and that requisite of every museum: the town's telephone switchboard. Next to some well-used saddles is a rack of barbed wire samples, 200 varieties in all. Amazing, when you think about it. If one thing tamed the West, it was barbed wire. But I had no idea it took so many different kinds.

Perko's was one of the few restaurants to survive a 6.7-magnitude earthquake that hit Coalinga in the late afternoon of May 2, 1983. In forty-five seconds, most of downtown was wiped out. Fifty-four buildings. Three hundred homes were also destroyed. Luckily, there were no deaths. Some people remember Perko's as the only normal spot in their lives afterward.

"We could come in here, have a nice meal, and the girls would smile like everything was OK, even though they were working fifteen-hour days. If you couldn't pay for your meal, that was OK, too," Bill Delco remembered, as we sat together at Perko's lunch counter. "Within minutes after the quake, the sky was full of airplanes. I haven't seen so many since Iwo Jima. We were pulling folks out of the rubble, and those news people were buzzing around making so much racket we could hardly hear each other," Bill recalls, with obvious bitterness.

Downtown Coalinga is rebuilt. Perko's, at the corner of Elm and Polk, now faces a McDonalds across the street and a traffic signal in front, the only one in town. Attached to the back of Perko's is Del's Odessa Bar-B-Que. "Del" is Delbert Geer, near age seventy, who shows up at 6:00 every morning "because I don't want to miss anything."

Outside Del's, under spreading shade trees, rests a 100-year-old hay rake and a barbecue grill the size of a grand piano. From mid-morning on, meaty ribs and beef tri-tips cover the grill. Meat drippings, hissing and sizzling when they hit the white-hot mesquite, create an odoriferous billboard that makes even a full stomach growl.

Inside Del's—actually a covered patio—grows a tree. Its trunk is a foot and a half in diameter. Del figures the tree has seniority, since it's older. So there it is, sticking through the roof. Picnic benches with red-checked tablecloths surround it. Del is in bib overalls, long sleeves, and an apron, apparently oblivious to the ninety-degree heat. He talks to everyone.

The world discovered Coalinga in 1968, when Interstate 5 opened, Del said. "The San Francisco-Los Angeles crowd and truckers from all over were suddenly as close as eighteen miles. Volkswagens used to come in off the highway in meltdown condition. Nobody here had parts for German cars then."

My last night in Coalinga, I camped in town by Olsen Park. There, some remarkably good ballplayers were fighting out a doubleheader. They played nearly to midnight. I guess most of the crowd stayed to the end, but not me. I went off to bed. I had promised Del that I would meet him before seven for some Odessa-brewed coffee. With the coming of a new day, I did not want to miss anything.

33

Searching for Main Street

Taft, California

Taft, about a hundred miles south of Coalinga on Highway 33, has one main street, two that really could be, and another that really is. Kern Street has the town's only stoplight, the bowling alley, McDonalds, two banks, and the city hall.

Center Street has the Fox Theater, two more banks, the office of the Taft Daily Midway Driller, and Ong's Chinese Cafe & Vacuum Cleaner Repair & Gift Shop.

Main Street, on the other hand, has fewer stop signs, the United Pentecostal Church (with only one window), and the empty Pioneer Mercantile Company Building. Obviously, Main Street is not the "main" one.

Tenth is definitely the busiest street at this time of the morning. Its two delis are doing a brisk business in coffee-to-go and Lotto tickets.

The day is an hour old and the sidewalks are empty, except for a lone gentleman on Center Street. He wears a white shirt and tie and carries a pouch of Watchtower magazines.

"This probably should be Main Street," he said, "That is, if you are naming the street because it is the main one." He pointed out that Center Street has angled parking and trees that come up through grated holes in the fancy, red-brick sidewalks, plus the J.C. Penney Store.

"Do you know we have an East and a West North Street?" he asked.

"Well, that makes sense, I guess."

"You think so? It's confusing as the dickens. If you're renaming streets in Taft, start with those two."

We laughed and parted company. I headed up East North, squinting into the sun that would bring the temperature here to ninety degrees by noon.

Having arrived at dusk last night and camped by the park next to the city hall, curiosity had me dressed and out of my motorhome before dawn.

This California oil town, population 6,000, has seen more prosperous times. But it is still the heart of the largest oil-producing region in the Lower Forty-eight.

A line of five newspaper racks in front of Jo's Family Restaurant on Kern Street might just as well be a billboard that says: "Everyone eats breakfast here." Most of the booths in Jo's are in pairs, with nothing more than salt shakers and pepper shakers and maybe a bottle of ketchup to interfere with the flow of conversation between them. My booth neighbors were Pat and Harold Hunt.

"Nobody had air-conditioning then," Pat said. "We took a box, open at both ends, draped wet gunnysacks over it, and blew air through with a fan."

Harold added, "We cool our house today with a swamp cooler. Same principle."

Pat was born here in 1928, when the whole town worked for the oil companies. Then over 2,300 wooden derricks peppered the hills around Taft, and gushers of 10,000 barrels a day were still coming in.

"As a kid, I would go to sleep at night by the noise of the oil pumps that were almost in our backyard. They would go bang and then chug-chug about five times, then bang again." The bang was the power stroke of a one-cylinder, gas engine. The chug was its two flywheels going around and around, using up the energy from the bang. "Each pump had its own rhythm. The night they stopped, I couldn't sleep," Pat remembered.

Eventually electric motors replaced the noisy, "hit-and-miss" engines. The wooden derricks are gone, too.

It took five men five days to build a 108-foot-tall derrick. Just the demand for timbers to build them made Taft the second-largest freight-receiving station in California in the early 1900s. The Sunset Railroad that ran thirty miles between Taft and Bakersfield was then the most profitable line in the world.

"When my daddy came here from Ireland, this town was like a rowdy mining camp," Pat continued. "I remember the Brass Rail Bar on Main Street had its windows broken out so many times they bricked them all in, except for one small one they left for ventilation."

"And it's now a Pentecostal Church?"

She looked surprised. "Looks like a bank vault, doesn't it? Whiskey was cheap. Beer and soft drinks were almost unheard of, probably because it took ice to cool them. There was little of that. Drinking water was shipped in. It sold for more than crude oil. They drilled water wells but just got more oil."

It all started with the Lakeview Gusher that erupted nearby on March 14, 1910. For a year and a half, this geyser of black gold poured out 50,000 barrels a day before anyone figured out how to cap it. There were many more, but none rivaled the Lakeview.

Pat looked at Harold's watch and announced that they must leave. It was time for Jeopardy.

California oilmen of the nineties wear ball caps that exhibit their individual loyalties, be it a ball team, a beer, where they hail from, or maybe a truck or tire maker. A Red Adair cap, which bears the embroidered likeness of the famous fighter of oil-well fires, is the most sought after in the oil patch, I was told.

The only Western-style hat I saw in Taft was at the post office. It was of black felt with a garland of sterling silver as a hatband. It was worn by a tall, straight man whose boots had silver tips matching those on his shirt collar. His shirt, too, was black with cowboy artifacts embroidered in red. His face and hands were those of a seventy-year-old, but he was probably younger. Several lost teeth and an Arkansas accent gave his speech a lilting lisp, maybe a guitar strum away from a country song.

"Gotta get to Pismo Beach by nightfall," he said, walking to his camper parked outside. His daughter and her daughter crowded into the front seat, which was already occupied by a dog.

As they backed from the curb, I asked a cityboy's question: "You got a card or something?"

"They call me Cowboy Dean. It's on the back," he said, pointing with a thumb to the rear of his camper.

Sure enough, reflective silver letters spelled out Love Me Tonight—Cowboy Dean—Country Classics Band. There were bumper stickers, too, but they were a blur before I could read them.

It was dark when I returned to my motorhome. I opened it to let in the cool night air. The park was quiet except for a couple of lovers who drove in to giggle and chase each other around the swings. I fell asleep without knowing if anyone got caught.

Just before dawn, water began pelting my motorhome. I jumped from my bed to close the roof vents to keep out the rain. False alarm. The automatic sprinklers in the park just had a long reach.

Leaving town, I stopped for coffee at McDonalds, the new early-morning hangout for Taft's old-timers since the Safeway closed. McDonalds gives free coffee to those over age sixty-five when they spend a dollar. So they buy three cookies, drink their free coffee for an hour or so, see their friends, and take the cookies home to their grandchildren. Great system. Everybody wins.

I sat with a group of five men who had qualified years ago for free coffee. Two were sipping through triangle-shaped holes in the plastic tops. They all talked.

"When haircuts went up to fifteen cents, I just didn't have one so often."

"You probably came out ahead over time. So the barber ended up the loser."

"But they say now they can't make it at five bucks. That's too much for seniors. We've got less hair for one thing."

"You know that new guy on Kern has a deal for seniors? He gives you the first and last haircuts free."

Silence. Some thoughtful swallows, too.

The same man continued, "I guess you just have to tell him it's your first time in there to get a free one."

Just then, a senior lady-customer walked by with a coffee-pot, but my attention was on the silent drama unfolding around me. One man mumbled something about decaf. Another struggled with a shaking hand to get the plastic top back on his cup.

It finally came.

"Yeah, but how do ya...or when do ya tell him? I mean, how do you know it's your last haircut?

"I guess ya don't. That's the way he makes his money."

They all laughed, but it seemed forced. After that, conversation slowed.

Back in my motorhome, I headed south on Highway 33 through oil fields where pumps stick up like cactus in the Arizona desert. I stopped in Maricopa to think for a while about which way to turn. I looked at the map. Either the heat of the valley or the cool of the coast. I headed west toward the Pacific.

34

Where Butterflies Spend the Winter

Pismo Beach, California

It's all one big, homogenized beach with sand hard enough to drive on. Its south end rolls into sand dunes. People used to run horses through the dunes. Some still do. But off-road vehicles are more popular now. You can rent one at the end of Pier Street without even getting your toes out of the sand.

California's Pacific Coast Highway runs parallel to the beach. Tourist haunts, groves of eucalyptus and Monterey pine, and pricey RV parks line both sides of the road. The towns of Grover Beach and Pismo Beach run together here. Apparently, identity is not a big issue, nor is competition. A Pismo Beach T-shirt can be bought in Grover Beach, and vice versa. Roadrunner beach towels cost the same in either place.

Pismo clams made this place famous for a while. Commercial fishermen once harvested as many as 45,000 a day. A few years of this, coupled with the appetites of sea otters, have about wiped out Pismo's namesake mollusk.

It's butterflies now. Although the interest in butterflies will never surpass that of the clams, their numbers may have already. From late November through March, millions of migrating monarch butterflies settle near here and at Pacific Grove, farther up the coast.

I think monarch butterflies are the greatest mystery of nature. They spend their winter here, then fly a couple thousand miles to Canada to spend the summer. There, they breed and die. But their offspring return here in the fall, to the very same trees. When these youngsters make their migratory flight, they know exactly where they are going.

The ageless attraction of Pismo Beach is its summer weather. When most of central California swelters in ninety-degree heat, here it can be in the low seventies or sixties, even foggy.

"I remember as a kid hearing talk about going to the beach with a horse and buggy. Roads were rough and went through walnut groves and around lettuce fields. It took them as long to get there as it takes me to drive to San Francisco," Gordon Bennett told me. His family goes back several generations in nearby Arroyo Grande, where his grandfather was the town's first mayor in 1911.

Midway between San Francisco and Los Angeles, Arroyo Grande is a century-old farming town of about 15,000 people. The trees and lettuce fields that Gordon spoke of are gone, replaced with people and their houses. The city limits of Arroyo Grande and the beach towns along the Pacific Coast Highway now bump against each other.

Arroyo Grande dates back to when Mexico issued land grants here. It was their territory until 1848. The Pacific Coast Railway set up a depot here in 1882.

35

A Convex, Equilateral, Three-Sided Temple

Halcyon, California

Even before Arroyo Grande laid out its boundaries, the town of Halcyon sprouted in its midst. With 125 people now, Halcyon is a square town of 95 acres.

A group from Syracuse, New York, with common religious beliefs established Halcyon in 1903.

They built a single-story, triangular-shaped temple here 20 years later. A 7-foot-wide porch and 36 white pillars surround it. Each pillar is 7 feet tall and 13 inches in diameter. These numbers all have significance, especially when added together and divided by each other.

The temple owns most of the houses in town. To live here, you don't have to belong to the temple. Only half of the people in Halcyon do. They are a low-profile group, with no strict rules or roles.

Eleanor Shumway is the guardian in chief of the Temple of the People. "I'm the minister, the mayor, the whole thing," she joked. We met in the post office and store, Halcyon's only commercial enterprise, and walked to her office across the street, above the town library. Among its racks of books, the library features a 700-cassette collection of old-time radio shows.

While Eleanor and I visited, another lady entered the office. Her name was Barbara. I think she is Eleanor's secretary, probably part-time. With a worldwide membership of fewer than 200 people, I don't suspect the guardian in chief of the temple needs much of a staff. Barbara volunteered to show me around.

"No street lights or sidewalks here, did you notice?" Barbara asked as we reached the temple. "Go around to the front door. I will let you in."

I started around the convex, equilateral, 3-sided temple, past 3 equal doors and the 36 pillars. Back where I started, I stopped. I heard footsteps on the porch coming around one of the triangular points of the temple.

"Which door is the front door?" I asked. Barbara came through it, looking for me.

Inside, she pointed out 26 windows, each having 8 panes of glass. Barbara read from a brochure: "Each clerestory window forms 6 squares, plus 8 triangles, equaling 14, or 2 times 7."

She offered me the brochure.

"I better have it," I confessed. "I never get things right the first time."

36

Adventures on a Narrow-Gauge Speeder

Arroyo Grande, California

Back in my motorhome, I headed north up Halcyon Road and hooked a right on Grand. It passes over U.S. 101, which splits Arroyo Grande in two. Grand there becomes Branch Street, the main street of Arroyo Grande Village, where this town started. Buildings along here were built in the 1880s.

Down the street is the county's last remaining one-room schoolhouse. It served the town until 1957. Another one-roomer, a block off Branch, is the Hoosegow, built as the village lockup in 1906. It still serves the town, but mostly just as a place for visitors to look at.

The "Village" is a good example of what many small towns—and big ones, too—are doing to save their historic main streets.

They have been wilting in this country for decades. If they wither and die, we have only ourselves to blame. If they do, we all lose a tangible piece of our legacy. Already, there is precious little left.

The villain, of course, is progress. Perpetual and unstoppable. Every generation embraces those highly visible advancements of the American lifestyle. Granted, our acceptance may not be to our ultimate betterment. Often, just because they are here, we accept them.

Maybe the whole thing began when folks were riding buggies from here to Pismo Beach. Henry Ford created a car that made it easier to get there, and we taxpayers made roads that allowed us to get there quicker. Then Sears & Roebuck mailed us catalogs so that we didn't have to leave the house to shop. Trucks began using our new roads to deliver things to our door. So, who needs Main Street?

Here in Arroyo Grande Village, main-street merchants have not given up on the local shoppers. Their focus, however, is on the outsider, the traveling public, we tourists. The village is not the center of commerce it once was, but at least it is still here. The shops are independently owned, one-of-a kind businesses. Of all the buildings, it appears a saloon and the Hoosegow are the only two that retain their original function.

"The biggest building along there had the boiler for the Lewis Dehydration Plant," Gordon Bennett remembers. "They dehydrated pumpkins in there and made flour for pumpkin pies. It was packed in tin canisters, twelve pies to a canister. They shipped them out in boxcars. The railroad track went right through their building."

Started in 1921, the dehydration operation did not last long. A wagonload of overripe pumpkins hastened the demise of the company. "The already mushy pumpkins were stored near the boiler, Gordon recollected. "They rotted in a hurry and smelled up the whole town. My cousin and I got in there one time, after they had closed up, and took a drying cart. It was like a small flatcar, a speeder that ran on narrow-gauge track. We would ride it to school. Four kids could ride if two pushed. Together we pushed the postmaster up the track one time. He gave us some stamps for the ride. I still have them."

"What about trains?" I asked.

"Trains quit running around 1937 or 1938. When the railroad found out about our speeder, that ended our railroading days."

Gordon led me to the yard behind his house. He pulled back a blue tarp. Under it was a narrow-gauge speeder, complete with a 6 1/2-horsepower gasoline engine.

"I didn't say that ended our railroading days forever."

37

Vandenberg's Thirty-Mile Beach

Pacific Coast Highway, California

The Pacific Coast Highway runs up the California coast, at times right at the ocean's edge. It passes by Los Angeles and San Francisco almost unnoticed. Then in towns like Newport Beach, Malibu, and Big Sur, it is the main street.

Officially called Highway 1, it was built when America's first cars needed roads to run on, a need that still determines how big the pavement gets. Where traffic mandated expansion, its personality as a two-lane scenic byway disappears, and its highway number becomes an also-ran. For example, once out of the Los Angeles maze, the northbound Pacific Coast Highway becomes U.S. 101, the first superhighway to San Francisco.

Beyond Santa Barbara at Gaviota, U.S. 101 turns north, and Highway 1 takes off again on its own. It swings inland for about fifty-five miles. Interestingly, this leaves coastal travel exclusively to Amtrak passengers on the tracks of the Southern Pacific Railroad. Highway 1 joins the ocean again farther up the coast at Grover City and Pismo Beach.

During its inland passage, Highway 1 goes through a couple of towns and cuts across a piece of Vandenberg Air Force Base. This space-flight and missile facility covers about

100,000 acres, including thirty miles of pristine coastline. Vandenberg is the biggest piece of ocean front property on the West Coast—probably the whole country—which is pretty much as it has always been. Part of the Pacific Missile Range, this piece of land that is bigger than some countries is more a physical barrier than anything. The Air Force does not traipse around on it like the Marine Corps or Army would, conducting training exercises and war games. Consequently, plants and wildlife live there relatively undisturbed.

I drove that inland passage, tracing El Jarco Creek on Highway 1 through long shadows and the rounded hills of the Santa Ynez Mountains. It was a lazy drive until just short of Lompoc. There the road took on shape, mostly curves, and the oncoming traffic seemed in a rush. The workday was ending. People were hurrying home.

38

Fog, Flowers, and Watermelon Seeds

Lompoc, California

Highway 1 took me into the center of Lompoc on Ocean Avenue. It is "subject to flooding," according to signs posted here. I envisioned that the person who named this street was on it one day when it flooded. Nothing so fanciful ever happened, of course. Ocean Avenue simply leads to the ocean, so I let it take me there.

It was nine miles to a place called Surf, which is little more than a railroad crossing. Fog was heavy. I parked, pulled on a jacket, and walked across the hard sand to the very edge of the American continent.

The surf rolled out an unbroken uproar like a waterfall, not an intermittent crash, as you might expect. I walked to a fence that closed off Vandenberg to the public. All this beachfront belongs to the Air Force. Seagulls hung in the air like satellites. They were watching me, I think. It's always curious when nature looks back.

Were it not for the defense needs of our country, this beach would surely be lined with high-rise condominiums and restaurants draped with fishnets and colored lanterns. Besides saving the world from a few disasters, our military has quietly preserved a piece of this Pacific frontier for generations to come. Obviously, it is not the Air Force's mission to be a land conservator. They get the job by default, and they do it well by just maintaining the fence.

Leaving the beach, I drove through a curtain of fog. The sun and Lompoc lay on the other side. This town is not a saltwater tourist mecca like the others tied to it by Highway 1. I don't suppose even a Snoopy beach towel is sold here, nor the knickknacks you buy a third cousin who is getting married. Lompoc appears focused on its own people, not those who come in off the highway. That was good enough for me. I decided to stay.

I stopped at the open-air farmers' market, a once-a-week occurrence at Ocean and I Streets. Vegetable shoppers clustered around the stands, shaded by umbrellas. Behind them, like a colorful stage prop, was a huge mural with sweeping waves of blues, reds, greens, and browns. It adorned the side of a building and took up half a block. Even an open door in the mural did not create a significant void in the picture. It was that big.

The Lompoc Murals Project began in 1988 and probably will go on forever. It now numbers twenty works of art on buildings around town, depicting events in local history. I found ten of them, all within five minutes of where I parked my motorhome. One alley is a two-walled, outdoor art gallery. The subjects ranged from people to porpoises.

I settled at the town's RV park next to the Santa Yenz River. There is no water in it, but a sign still warns of sudden flooding. Guess it could happen here, too, but not tonight.

The next morning, fog off the ocean made the day look chillier then it really was. Although the people in Lompoc can't see the ocean, their weather is controlled by it. An average high in July is seventy-one degrees; in January, it is sixty-four degrees.

This marine influence, with days beginning and ending in moisture-laden fog, has made the Lompoc Valley ideal for growing flowers. It has been the sole crop here for most of this century.

Darrel Schuyler has been here the whole time. "I am a third-generation farmer," Darrel said. "We grow flowers for seeds, not for funerals and things like that. But much of that seed production has now moved to Chile and China. The hottest crop here now is asparagus." I met Darrel in the Hi Restaurant, where he and a group of guys gather for coffee most mornings.

Every town has a place like the Hi. If one group activity remains exclusively male in this increasingly unisex world, it happens every morning in small-town America around Formica tables. Like an all-night poker game, the composition of the table changes one at a time.

"It takes two years to get a crop of asparagus," Darrel continued. "They cut it by hand and wrap it in a wet blotter that feeds it going to the market. And ya know where that market is, don't ya? It's Japan."

Then he told me just how hard it is to grow seedless-watermelon seeds. "It's so tough, they sell for $1,500 a pound."

"You mean a ton?" I was sure one of us had it wrong.

"No, a pound. That's about a quart jar full."

Before I could further pursue this question, we got sidetracked saying good-bye to the judge, who was leaving for court. Everyone was very courteous to the judge, the only man in the restaurant wearing a tie.

The fellow across the table changed the subject to diatomaceous earth. He mined it, which involves scraping it off the sides of mountains.

"It's used in filters. They call it diatomite. It's really a few million layers of a few million years worth of dead marine life, like crustaceans and algae," the miner explained. "Out of here, most of it goes to the brewing industry, but you see it too in swimming-pool filters."

The Lompoc Valley is the world's largest producer of diatomaceous earth. Obviously, this was ocean bottom eons ago. In spite of baking in the sun since then, the material is still 50 percent water, which is cooked out when it is processed.

Darrel drifted somewhere. I never got a chance to talk with him again. The price of seedless watermelon seeds still hounded me. I wanted to get it right. I spent the rest of the day working at it. My search led me all over town.

I drew a blank at the chamber of commerce. They made some phone calls, tried to help, but couldn't. I asked a lady at a plant nursery. She thought I was nuts, but referred me to the Bodger Seeds Company at the edge of town. They only know about flower seeds, and they showed me multiple bags of those. I even called the Santa Barbara County Growers Association. Their answer: "We don't grow melons in this county."

As a last resort, I logged on the Internet and tied into the Froese Seed Company in Albuquerque, New Mexico. Kathleen Froese wrote me that she sells seedless-watermelon seeds for 11 or 12 cents apiece to truck farmers. By the pound, they can run as high as $1,500, Kathleen wrote, but she sells them retail for about $750.

Glad that's over!

39

Servicetown, USA

Buellton, California

In a town known for ranching and a great recipe for pea soup, Buellton's Avenue of the Flags appears as a magnificent boulevard waiting for a city. With four lanes in each direction—two for driving, two for parking, and room for six more in a grassy meridian—it's a lavish main street for a town of 4,000 people, even in California. Each block has its own floodlit flagpole, from which the American flag is never lowered. On a summer day, the vehicle count on the avenue averages around thirty an hour. That's a mere trickle compared to what it once was.

" 'No way!' we told 'em. That was the first time, in 1948. They wanted to move the highway out of town so they could make it wider. Well, the highway was the town. We lived off it. In those days, Highway 101 was the direct route between Los Angeles and San Francisco. This was the first natural stop for those out of LA and the second stop for those coming south. We had eleven gas stations and a big sign: Welcome to Servicetown, USA."

Jack Mendenhall pulled a pen from the pocket of his plaid shirt and roughed out a map on a paper napkin. We sat in Mother Hubbard's Coffee Shop, on the Avenue of the

Flags, and are well into our third cup of coffee. A lady who overfilled the chair at the table next to us was spooning up the remains of her biscuits and gravy. Her tight wristwatch had almost disappeared around her beefy arm. She chided us for drinking so much coffee. "Bad for your heart and vessels," she scolded us with a Texas accent.

"Buellton is 150 miles from LA," Jack goes on. "That's about as far as a guy drove in a day. The road was two lanes, full of curves. The cars were slow."

Jack savored a special memory.

"When I started pumping gas, and I mean we literally pumped it, it was five gallons for a buck, including tax. Remember the old visual gas pumps? At night they were a thing of beauty."

A visual gas pump had a cylindrical, glass tank on top. The tank usually held ten gallons. An attendant pumped gas into the tank by hand. Gallon markers on the tank showed the customer exactly how much gas he or she got and what color it was. Some was blue-green or orange. Ethyl was usually red.

"Light from the globe on top would streak into the glass tank and filter through the gasoline, making the whole tank glow, almost shimmer. As the gasoline went out, air bubbled up through it. The bubbles were clear as crystal in a sea of orange or whatever. Who remembers that? Darn few, I'll bet."

I learned later that Jack is a collector of the old visual gas pumps and their colorful, lighted glass crowns. At age sixty-seven, he is also a race-car driver. He's done 219 miles per hour at Bonneville Flats.

I tapped on the map-napkin. "So, what happened in '48?"

"Well," Jack leaned back in his chair, "the businesses along the highway agreed to move their buildings back, at their expense, so the state could widen the road. What's more, they gave the state the land to do it. Pretty generous, eh? That worked fine until 1962. Then the state proclaimed that 101 was to be a divided highway and that it would bypass Buellton. We said, 'But you owe us from last time.' We wanted three interchanges into town and the old highway turned into a parkway, grass and all. They agreed, surprisingly. Later, we put up the flagpoles."

There is one tree on the parkway. It's a mature pine, about two stories tall. It was cut fresh from the nearby hills for the Christmas tree in 1970. They stuck it in the ground and wired it down as in years past. It was Jack's job, since he then owned the tow trucks in town, to lift the tree out and dispose of it after Christmas. He claims he forgot or got busy. By the time he got to it, the tree had sprouted new growth and apparently had taken root. It still stands where they stuck it in 1970. It is Buellton's perennial Christmas tree.

Slick travel brochures—the kind that overflow showy racks in tourist centers—call Buellton "the Gateway to the Santa Ynez Valley."

White wooden fences embroider pastures of prosperous cattle ranches and horse farms in the Santa Ynez Valley. The fields create a patch-work-quilt effect in the rolling hills of oak and eucalyptus. Carefully tended citrus groves and vineyards add a mix of pattern and color. Tucked away in the valley are three little towns, a lake, and seven wineries open for tours and tasting. The valley oozes with rural charm and is increasingly a retreat for the Los Angeles crowd seeking serenity and sanity. A few entertainment celebrities call it home. An ex-president did, too, until a few years ago.

The valley also has Solvang, a Danish community of about 5,000 residents that draws nearly that many tourists every day. They come to stroll through Old-World ambiance, to eat aebleskiver—a globe-shaped Danish pancake—and to buy rare, handmade items ranging from furniture to toys.

That Buellton is the valley's gateway is a geographic fact. But it is more than just a drive-through to Danish pastry and wine country. Aside from having a main street that could double as a golf course, Buellton is the home of California's most famous roadside restaurant. It dates to 1924, when two young immigrants arrived here with little more than a dream and Juliette Andersen's recipe for pea soup.

In those days, it wasn't vehicle count or competition that dictated where to locate an eatery for travelers, it was how many driving-hours since the last one. "The ranch town of Buellton was perfect, the first natural stop," as Jack said.

Electricity came to the valley about the same time the Andersens did. Anton, who had been a chef in Denmark and New York, was so proud of his electric stove that he named his restaurant after it: Andersen's Electric Café. Within a few years, electric cafés were as common as the name Andersen. So, Anton hung a new name on his place when he added a twenty-room inn: Buellton Hotel Café. In 1939, the name evolved to Andersen's Valley Inn.

Although he had built his business on his wife's pea soup, Andersen had not yet hit on a catchy name that sported his café's specialty. But his friends had. Around town, Andersen—always seen in a white shirt and tie—was known as "Pea Soup." His café became Pea Soup Andersen's. Whether he made the decision or others made it for him doesn't matter. The name changed in 1947. Anyone who travels Highway 101 today knows it. Marketing genius or chance, the restaurant's name and the pea soup it dishes out bring in over a million and a half tourists a year to Buellton.

Although Juliette and Anton are long gone, Pea Soup Andersen's is still where it has always been, although it has changed owners a couple of times. It's twice its original size but still serves the same thick, green soup for $3.95, all you can eat.

"How much is that?" I asked former manager Jimmy Sanchez.

"The record is eighteen bowls," Jimmy replied. "The man who set that record came back once when I was a waiter. He could only handle thirteen then."

On a good day, Andersen's sells 500 to 600 gallons of pea soup. That is more than all the servings of wine, beer, coffee, and soft drinks combined.

Jimmy's father, Joe Sanchez, is the head chef. He started with Andersen's thirty-one years ago, five years before Jimmy was born. Joe and his kitchen crew make the soup the day before it is served, allowing it to simmer all night in eighty-gallon vats. "Carrots, celery, peas, and seasoning. That's all that's in it," Joe explained.

That simple recipe of Juliette's and the town's around-the-clock commitment to the traveling public, put Buellton on the map long before the Santa Yenz Valley began luring tourists with wine, tranquillity, and a piece of old Denmark. It was at least a quarter century after Andersen dished up his millionth bowl of green soup and Mendenhall pumped his millionth gallon of orange gasoline that the trendy valley even had a need for a "gateway."

Now they pass off old Servicetown USA, as a mere point of entry, a drive-by window. Another facade is fabricated. Tourists revel in it. We who journey through do our best to understand it.

Part IV

California — Arizona — Utah

40

Home for a Visit

Rancho Palos Verdes, California

It has become a semiannual ritual, my returning home to off-load clothes of the season past and to take on those appropriate for the next one. But this visit marked a milestone: I have been rummaging around the country now for two years, 28,000 miles alone in a motorized condo.

I have lived here in Palos Verdes, south of Los Angeles, for twenty-five years, which is as long as I have lived in any one place. I guess it is home. This is where my kids grew up. Both of them, Chris and Kathy, are grown now. In fact, Kathy recently made me a picture-toting grandfather.

Serene and comfortable, this gorgeous Palos Verdes Peninsula is surprisingly isolated and disconnected from the craziness of the big city. It is a marvelous place to live, a community of wonderful people. For the past couple of years, however, Palos Verdes for me has been just a closet and a mailbox.

Back to living a conventional, rooted life here—albeit temporarily—I crossed paths at Hughes Market with a veterinarian friend of mine. He, too, has a motorhome and travels alone. Well, not really. He takes along his 130-pound English mastiff.

"The dog sleeps on the floor. I'm stepping around him most of the time," my friend said as we walked to the parking lot. "But you can't beat the companionship, if you don't mind stumbling over it."

He could see that I was listening well. Then he mentioned a stray female pup that was being fussed over by all the people in his clinic. A young girl who works for him, assisted by her boyfriend, rescued her from a busy city intersection. He told me that the dog was traumatized by the traffic, too scared to move, which probably saved her life. So to get her mind off her trauma, her rescuers took her to McDonalds for lunch. "I can't speak to her early days, but her last few have been the good life," he said.

Advertising for her owner the past week had not surfaced one.

"After I bring her up to code, she will be a perfect dog for a guy like you. She is mostly lab, probably won't get over sixty pounds. Not a big dog."

Sure, not big by his standards.

My friend suggested that I take her home for the weekend to see how we got along. We got along just as well as he expected. I got a traveling companion. He got rid of a hungry freeloader who was taking up kennel space.

Although she is black with white trim, white paws, and a white chest, I named her "Rusty" after a golden Labrador retriever that my family had when I was a kid.

From the beginning, Rusty showed a desperate desire to please. I think there were some dark experiences in Rusty's early days that have made this instinct powerful indeed. Which makes me wonder if a young dog, traumatized by feeling hopelessly lost or abandoned, does not spend the rest of its life showing its appreciation for being rescued. Rusty seems to. She tries extremely hard to do everything right.

Rusty came with no apparent house training but picked that up quickly. I credit the motorhome with that success. Because it has limited space, I think she sees it as her house, her crate, as the dog books call it. Given a choice, a dog prefers not to dirty its house. And I give Rusty plenty of choices, all of them just a couple of steps away.

It was time to leave this sedentary existence, time to flee the chaotic traffic that Rusty feared and I hated. We headed into the unknown while it was still dark, not knowing what to expect from each other. The idea of having company on this journey felt especially good. Who knows what Rusty thought of it? For her it was a totally new adventure.

41

The Year's Longest Day

Sheep Hole Summit, California

I wanted an early start on the desert, a geographic mass to
be dealt with for all the eastbound traffic out of Los Angeles. This is the first day of summer, the longest day of the
year, which means the sun has more time to cook this desert
and set heat records.

Rusty and I left Interstate 10 near Palm Springs and
climbed north toward the town of Morongo Valley. Covering
the high ridges on both sides of Highway 62 are wind farms:
hundreds, maybe thousands, of steel towers topped with
multi-bladed wind turbines. A faddish tax-shelter gimmick of
the 1980s, they are spinning in a strong wind today, presum-
ably generating electricity. As an investment, I have heard that
they are a disaster. Quite often, they don't spin at all.

Residents out here are known to tell out-of-towners that
the wind turbines are here to blow the smog out of Los
Angeles. I suspect the turbines might be as successful doing
that as what they are touted to do.

Highway 62 straightens out, levels, and becomes the
Twentynine Palms Highway. It is named for the town on its
eastern end, after it passes through Yucca Valley and Joshua
Tree. Signs depict the territory well, like Dig Your Own

Cactus—39 Cents, Sunburst Park, and Desert-High this and that. One exception is the Seahorse Saloon, the only one in the desert, I bet. Space is plentiful. The population is sparse. Growth is apparently no problem here, unless they want more of it.

A couple of ninety-degree turns and we are on Amboy Road, rolling through shallow dips in the open desert. Where every side road joins Highway 62 stood rows of mailboxes. Obviously, people live out there somewhere, far off these side roads, but they must be living very close to the ground. Signs of human life in the desert may take many forms: a cluster of trees, the sun reflecting off glass or metal, maybe a string of telephone poles. I saw none of these.

Wheel tracks in the sand and some narrow roads snaking up the sides of the Sheep Hole Mountains tell of people. Otherwise, nothing man-made breaks the landscape. There are no crops, no livestock, not even fences. Living on it maybe, but nobody is living off this land.

Cresting Sheep Hole Summit at 2,368 feet, we view the downside, looking north. Off in the distance, twenty-four miles, stretchs Old Route 66 and the town of Amboy, indistinguishable in the haze.

Dropping to the desert floor, the temperature in the motorhome quickly rose to 105 degrees. Rusty let me know that this was something new for her. Her tongue dripping, she hunted for a cool spot on the floor. Too late to turn on the air conditioner. It would not make a dent in this scorched air. So I opened the windows and roof vents and just let the desert blow through the motorhome. It was hot, but the superheated air was dry, which made it bearable.

The road passed over the cracked and crusty white bottom of a dry lake. It reminded me of Devil's Golf Course in Death Valley, which is solid salt—jagged, sharp, and hard as steel. Here the salt is being commercially removed, but not this day. No salt is worth mining in this heat.

Just before reaching Route 66, now called the National Trails Highway, a crossing gate stopped us at the railroad tracks. Rusty came alive. I discovered that she loves to watch trains but hates the whistle. This train was long and whistled very little. No doubt, this was the highlight of Rusty's day.

42

Route 66

Amboy, California

Turning onto Route 66, the road sign announced Amboy, population twenty, founded in 1858. Clustered in Amboy's only shade, in front of a café, were a couple dozen Harley-Davidson motorcycles. They looked fresh from the showroom. Their owners were sucking water from plastic bottles, packing ice in coolers and mopping their heads where their helmets had been.

One rider, an attractive gal from Minneapolis, told me that they were a few of the 430 Harley owners who were riding from Milwaukee to the Pacific Ocean at Santa Monica on what remains of the original Route 66. Two riders from France air-shipped their "hogs" over here just to make this ride. They spoke of the huge interest in Europe in America's "Mother Road," calling it the route of the greatest human migration in the twentieth century. I am sure they are right. These Frenchmen knew more about this piece of Americana than I did.

I was looking for Buster. In my travels along Route 66 here in California, old-timers have spoken of Buster often. They said he tells great stories about the thirties and forties, when this historic road through Amboy was a way of life, not a mere 2,448-mile stretch of cement that ran from Chicago to Los Angeles. Buster was here then. Over the last few years, I must have stopped in Amboy a half-dozen times looking for him, but we have never met. Buster owned the café with the much-sought-after shade, where the gas pumps are. Buster built a row of white, boxlike tourist cabins, which later grew into a motel. Sometime after World War II, I guess, he added a tall neon sign and a motel lobby fronted with floor-to-ceiling glass. The best I could tell, he had given up on the motel, except its lobby, where his wife had an art gallery.

Buster's roadside business is all there is to Amboy, if you exclude the eight-to-noon post office across the road and, of course, the busy tracks of the Burlington Northern–Santa Fe Railroad. Otherwise, this is textbook desert, as in hot, vast, barren.

Glancing toward the motel lobby, I noticed that racks of white T-shirts embossed with Route 66 decals had replaced the oil paintings. And the sign on the café now read Roy's Texaco, Welcome Travelers on Route 66. Something was amiss. Commercializing his heritage was not Buster's style.

The guy behind the counter in the café was a walking display right off the racks in the lobby—shirt, hat, belt buckle, even a "Get Your Kicks on Route 66" button. He broke the news. "They sold out and moved to Twentynine Palms."

As I turned to leave, he added, "Yeah, Buster is history."

I wanted to yell something about the volumes of history that left with him. But I knew the human billboard behind the counter would not, probably could not, comprehend it.

Rusty hopped inside the motorhome. I told her we had probably seen the last of Amboy. She wagged her tail in agreement.

I thought that someday I might stop in Twentynine Palms and look up Buster. But how would I do that? I didn't even know his last name.

43

The One-Man Post Office

Essex, California

Headed east on the great "Migrant Way," sparks of sun shot from polished chrome and steel as we met a continuing parade of oncoming motorcycles. The rumble that rolls with a group of Harleys is probably as well rooted and traditionally American as this road.

Route 66 was busy well beyond the Depression years, the years of the "greatest human migration," as the Frenchmen called it. In the 1930s, this road was filled with people bound for California, escaping layoffs in the Midwest and dust storms on the Great Plains. Later, after World War II, touring America via Route 66 became a national pastime. Neon lights, billboards, and mechanical cowboys twirling lariats enticed tourists to the latest innovation of American's innkeepers: the motor court. Roadside vendors vied for the traveling trade with snake pits, live buffaloes, and Indian dances. And a bottle of Coke came out of machines for a nickel.

At Essex, a sign on the edge of town set the population at 100. Jack Howard shook his head. "I think it's more like 50 people—maybe 60 on the holidays."

Jack sat in the tiny stone post office, which had just enough floor space for a table and his chair. I hunched over

(I'm not tall) so I could see Jack and talk to him through the thin bars at the stamp window.

"You must work alone."

"Yep, you bet I do. Couldn't do it any other way. Been postmaster here since 1967."

"Got any Elvis stamps?"

He laughed. "Strange that you should ask. I remember selling my last sheet of those to a tourist from Holland."

Jack got up, walked outside, and lit a cigarette. "You can't smoke any more in a federal building. Did ya know that? But I don't mind. It's nice to get out."

He looked up and down the road. Nothing moved.

"Hmm," Jack grunted and drew on his cigarette. "The old road is getting busier. People over the mountain have discovered it's a quick way to get to Laughlin and the river. This post office, the diner, and the garage next door, which shut down years ago, were built in 1932 by a guy from Phoenix. He broke down here and decided it was a good place to start a business fixing cars.

"My wife was born here. She remembers stories about the Okies coming through in the thirties. What wasn't in their car was strapped to the sides, things like water bags and a mattress or two. She's the schoolteacher here. One room, one teacher, all grades through junior high."

Jack and I walked over to an Indian couple whose car had broken down. Luckily, they were parked in the shade, under the canopy of the deserted garage. Jack stayed and talked. I returned to my motorhome.

I opened a Pepsi. Rusty and I walked across the road and into the desert a ways. The desert, more than any other terrain, shows its age, the passage of time. Vegetation does not cover the eons of erosion by wind and storm. Everywhere is rock, the world's oldest thing, and tawny grit that was once rock. Even desert creatures come from a time older than their woodland cousins. In response to this arduous existence, many have retained their prehistoric coverings of lapped scales.

We returned to find the post office closed. Nobody was around. If this stretch of Old Route 66 was getting busier, as Jack said, there certainly was no sign of it today.

I gave Rusty her dinner and got back on the road. The low sun turned Castle Dome behind me into a silhouette. Ahead lay Interstate 40 and Arizona. Way out there, on the tracks of the Burlington Northern–Santa Fe, were the head-lights of a freight train coming from Needles. I thought about Fred Myers, the railroad brakeman I met there. Was he on that train? And how are the friends of the Harvey House in Needles?

Fond memories of people I meet along this journey create a hollow that grows as this nomadic life ages. I think of them and often wonder how their lives are going. Though my time with them is short, I remember it well. It's like waving to a conductor passing in a caboose. Twenty seconds of coming together. Then, in an instant, it's over. Again I am alone, watching the train disappear to nothing.

Rusty will bring some camaraderie and maybe a fresh outlook to this lonely lifestyle. I can use it.

44

The Sun's Hot Grip

Kingman, Arizona

Finding cool air in Arizona in the summer is a simple numbers game: the higher the elevation, the lower the temperature. Arizona has no monopoly on this, of course. But for me, on this scorching day in June, it is a glorious reawakening to the laws of physics.

We are camped in Bullhead City, down by the river. When the sun is toasting the Southwest, it's baking Arizona and blistering Bullhead. It is hot. The water coming into the motorhome, solar heated in the hose outside, is almost hot enough for instant coffee and perfect for washing dishes. I got cooler water for drinking out of the insulated hot-water tank. One day of this is enough.

Before the sun could get a grip on the day, I called Rusty from under the motorhome. Her tongue was close to dragging on the ground. I packed up, pulled the plug, and headed for the town on my map of Arizona with the highest elevation: Flagstaff, at 6,905 feet.

Comfortably air-conditioned but fighting a crosswind on Interstate 40, I hadn't planned to stop in Kingman. But the exit sign read Andy Devine Avenue. What did I expect from a street named for a cowboy-movie sidekick? I don't know, but we were on it. Anyway, it perked up Rusty.

We stopped at a grassy park with a steam locomotive as its centerpiece. Rusty rolled and reveled in the cool grass.

A guy who looked like a cowboy hobbled by, dragging a half-leg cast, and then hobbled back. His expression resembled Rusty's when she knows I am hiding a ball in my pocket. I could see it was coming: the last two chapters of his life, for sure, unless I distracted him from the start. So I asked him about Andy Devine.

He paused. He had to think hard. Two fingers parted his unkempt mustache. "Well, he was born here, you know, and growed up to be a bell-hop in the hotel is what I heard. Beyond that, I'm not sure who the guy was."

Then he started on something about which he was an expert: big rocks and bad horses. It took them both, conspiring concurrently, to break his leg.

Rusty voluntarily hopped in the motorhome. She had heard enough, too. I wished the cowpuncher good health. He preferred that title to cowboy. We continued east.

Kingman lies just about in the middle of the longest stretch of Old Route 66 that still exists, about 140 miles of it. Route 66 was the main street of small towns like this all along its route. That is how it got yet another nickname: "Main Street of America."

In 1938, Route 66 became the first cross-country highway in the United States to be completely paved. Construction of our interstate highway system began in 1956. Here in Arizona, parts of Route 66 were still carrying cross-country traffic almost three decades later. That is, until Interstate 40 pulled the last of it off the old Main Street of America.

45

The Grand Canyon vs. Route 66

Williams, Arizona

Though radio reception is scratchy along this stretch of Interstate 40, I was hearing news of wildfires in the Coconino National Forest around Flagstaff. It's said to contain the largest stand of ponderosa pine in the world. Reports of road closures caused me to rethink my plans as I approached Williams.

Smoke hanging over the tree line, albeit twenty miles ahead, made my decision easy. Williams, elevation 6,752, would do just fine.

It's a tourist town of 2,500 people. For the better part of this century, it has exploited its proximity to Grand Canyon National Park. Visited by over 5 million people a year, the Grand Canyon is America's number one tourist attraction not made by Disney. The Grand Canyon's popular South Rim fifty-nine miles north up Highway 64, is an easy drive from Williams.

I got the impression that Williams would include the Grand Canyon in its city limits if it could. The chamber of commerce, in effect, already has. It calls itself the Williams–Grand Canyon Chamber of Commerce. Even the town's century-old newspaper has stretched its name to include Grand

Canyon, hyphenated between Williams and News. The town's title is "Gateway to the Grand Canyon." This is no mere nickname, casual slogan, or debatable claim. No way! Williams owns it. And no place else in this state better use it, because they have copyrighted it. It's their trademark. It even ends with the little circled R, for registered.

Obviously, tourism is serious business here. Their season is short. Merchants catering to out-of-towners who don't make it between Memorial Day and Labor Day probably won't get a second chance. Of the 1,316 motel and bed-and-breakfast rooms here, most of them are empty all winter, either by intent or default.

The town's historic relevance is a lesser draw for tourists than the Grand Canyon, but if you count the downtown stores involved in its merchandising, it's a much bigger deal. Of course, it's the "Mother Road" again, Route 66.

"The last stoplight on Route 66 between Chicago and Los Angeles was right outside our door. It was a constant car-accident and horn-blowing caravan those final months before they opened I-40. The sound of a half-dozen semis with jake-brakes roaring and tires screeching was quite a clamor. And it happened, I think, every time the light turned red. When the light changed, it was almost as bad with everybody in low-gear unison," John Holst told me.

"The day they opened the interstate I will never forget. People walked out in the middle of the street and just stood there, marveling at the emptiness. I did it myself. It was like somebody threw a switch on the track and sent the train in a different direction."

John calls himself an innkeeper now. He operates the Red Garter Bed and Bakery. It's in a building on Old Route 66 that he has given a magnificent new life. The labor has consumed seventeen years, the better part of his. "Some guys want a '67 Chevy. I always wanted a classic old building to rehab," he said.

While enjoying fine coffee in John's ground-floor bakery, he showed me pictures and spoke of his reborn building with the enthusiasm of a proud parent.

Upstairs, now guest rooms, was once a bordello with eight cribs, each ten feet square with twelve-foot ceilings. The two front rooms, John said as we walked through them, were the "best-girl rooms." Their windows look out over the railroad tracks across the street, which were the focus of Williams around the turn of the century. The windows made promotion and soliciting easy for the girls in those front rooms, which may account for their occupants being the "best" girls. Then again, who decided who was best, and how was it determined? John would not even guess.

Downstairs was a saloon, one of many along this saloon row, and an opium den. Attached to the back of the building is a two-story outhouse. That is, the toilet seats are on the second floor. The visual imagery here is just too real to pass up. Yes, it was a long drop.

The Grand Canyon Railway now uses the railroad tracks across the street. Second to Amtrak, it may be the most advertised railroad in the United States, surely in Arizona. It runs sixty-five miles to and from the Grand Canyon every day, except Christmas and the day before. It was built in 1901 to offer tourists an alternative to the eight-hour stagecoach ride from Flagstaff to the South Rim. It outlived the stagecoach but could not compete with the automobile. It quit running in 1968.

Although Amtrak does little more than blow a whistle going by here today, all the old passenger trains once stopped in Williams. There was even a Harvey House: the Fray Marcos. Everyone knows that Harvey Houses were a chain of railside hotels and dining rooms that spanned the country with the Santa Fe Railroad. Of course, you know that.

Service on the Grand Canyon Railway, with an old steam engine in the lead, was restarted in 1989. The depot is the original 1908 Fray Marcos. This "ride into history," as they call it, hauls about 150,000 people a year. The daylight trip to the South Rim takes a little over two hours each way.

A subtle but important benefit of the railroad is that it cuts back on the vehicle traffic at the South Rim, where there is little room for it anyway. A few eccentrics still pound the podium and say that we should never have opened the Grand Canyon to cars in the first place. Some say we should never have opened it to people. But those kind are hard to find around Williams.

46

"Little Hollywood"

Kanab, Utah

North of the Grand Canyon, the flat, empty mesas of Arizona suddenly give way to the rugged ridges of Utah. Sudden is the change of scenery. As if decreed by the two state legislatures. Bound by the Colorado River to the south and east, and elsewhere by the borders of Utah and Nevada, this 12,000-square-mile mesa is called the Arizona Strip. The only sign of life on it—human or otherwise—is this road.

Around 1895, half a million cattle grazed this flat land to death. For reasons known only to nature, the vegetation never has recovered. Not yet, anyway.

Passing into Utah on Highway 89, I immediately entered Kanab. This town lived its first fifty years practically isolated. It is still alone, but now easily accessible. Kanab is located in the true outback of southwest Utah, just two miles from the Arizona line, in the most uninhabitable terrain in the continental United States. And the most gorgeous.

Wagon trains didn't pass this way. Roaming migrants who settled the far-out places of the West never happened on it, either. Why? For a couple of big reasons: the gorge of the Colorado River is on two sides, the peaks of the Wasatch and Rocky Mountains on another. Even the arrival of the cross-country railroads did not make it less remote. In fact, Kanab for two decades held the dubious national distinction as the incorporated town the greatest distance from a railroad.

Apparently, nobody came here by choice except the Indians. Mormon settlers were sent here from Salt Lake City in 1858. They built a fort in 1863, which was attacked so many times that they abandoned it four years later, fearing an Indian war. Another group of Mormons arrived as missionary-colonizers. They established a permanent peace with the Indians and founded Kanab in 1870.

The name Kanab was here before white settlers. It is an Anglicized form of the Paiute word for "willows". The Indians gave the name to the nearby creek with lush willow trees along its banks.

With high sandstone cliffs edging it on three sides and an unproductive desert on the other, early Kanab was never prosperous. They raised sheep and cattle on mountain pastures, but mostly just hung on.

With every sunrise, folks here knew they lived in a magical place, where nature's wonders extended far over the horizon. They also knew that their future lay in sharing it. They simply waited for the automobile to catch on so it could happen. With paved roads, Kanab willingly gave up another unsought title: the most inaccessible incorporated town of more than 500 people in the United States.

Highways were only a part of the story. In the 1920s, a couple thousand miles away in Washington, D.C., Kanab's destiny was being sketched on maps and chalkboards. Politicians were extolling the wonders of wilderness and designating national parks and monuments in Utah and Arizona. As a result, 2 million acres of geological marvels were set aside for public use. After the boundaries were drawn and the political dust settled, the folks in Kanab looked around them. The three roads out of town all lead to one or more of these natural wonders that Washington was going to open, promote, clean, and protect. None was more than a two-hour drive from here.

On the other side of the continent, at about the same time, a new industry was making a boomtown out of Hollywood, California. Westerns were in vogue, both in this country and overseas. Movie studios needed filming locations that offered wide-open spaces. Obviously, they also wanted spectacular backdrops and varied landscapes. The area around Kanab was perfect. Today, Kanab likes to be known as "Little Hollywood." Starting in 1924, with the Tom Mix movie Deadwood Coach, over fifty films have been made here.

Consistent with its past, Kanab was not just happened-upon or discovered like Lana Turner, making malts in a drug-store on Hollywood Boulevard. Kanab had to work for recognition. Two local men, the Parry brothers, were sent from Kanab as ambassadors to Hollywood with a packet of pictures. They called themselves "scenery salesmen."

The bonanza started with a production company from Metro-Goldwyn-Mayer headed by Wallace Berry. The movie was The Bad Man of Brimstone. MGM was back two years later making Billy the Kid with Robert Taylor. The word soon got around Hollywood that Kanab was not just a picture-perfect location but also had people who could produce whatever else a movie company needed.

Everybody got into the act, which paid very well. Two Mormon bishops here worked as cowboy extras and stunt riders. Townswomen were stand-ins. One even doubled for Maureen O'Hara. The mayor had an almost steady job as a chauffeur for movie directors. The sheriff doubled as a location-camp cook. City councilmen worked as horse wranglers. The town barber turned out to be a good actor and even got speaking parts. Many days a sign hung in his shop window: Working on a Movie. Back at 6:30.

Consequently, the people in Kanab paid grocery bills that they had owed for months and paid tax bills that had been delinquent for years. The winter of 1938, the year MGM came to town, was the first one that every Kanab youngster attended school. In the past, many simply never had clothes to go to school.

The movie companies rescued Kanab. A blight was rapidly destroying the nearby grasslands, without which local cattle ranches could not survive. Without the ranches, Kanab had nothing but scenery.

How the West Was Won finished shooting here in 1979. Since then a few film crews have come to shoot commercials and TV episodes, but Kanab's days in the movies may be over. Westerns are not made much anymore.

Utah 89 runs through town and makes a sharp turn by the Parry Lodge. It is a beautiful, white-pillared, colonial-style hotel built by Whit Parry in 1931. Better than anyone else, Parry knew from his tenure as a scenery salesman that movie companies needed a nice place to stay. So he built one. In the lodge, I found just what I expected. The dining room, with hardwood floors and linen-covered tables, is called the "dining room of the stars." The lobby is walled with pictures of movie stars who stayed here. One is three times bigger than any other. It is "Duke," of course, John Wayne. He made four movies here. The last one, She Wore a Yellow Ribbon, was filmed in 1949.

Across the street is a yellow-wheeled stagecoach complete with a load of baggage on top. It's in front of Denny's Wigwam, which caters mostly to groups and bus tours. Denny's feeds them a "chuck wagon cookout" and in a side yard gives them a cowboy show rigged with abbreviated western movie sets. Tourists like to stand next to the movie sets and click pictures.

Wigwam owner Denny Judd, a fifth-generation Kanab rancher, said that Americans travel in cars while foreigners travel in buses. He figures those foreign visitors to his place outnumber Americans three to one. During my visit, a busload of Germans made it more like sixty to one.

All the handmade Indian items sold here come from tribes in Utah, neighboring Arizona, or New Mexico. It was satisfying to shop where "Native American" work is not done in China or Turkey or Mexico.

Kanab conducts the business of tourism like it should be done but seldom is. Obviously, residents have had decades to refine and perfect it. There are no garish, rough edges here, no tasteless promotions, no callous facades. Things are clean and tidy. People smile and are willing to chat, even about local trivia that they have been over hundreds of times. This freshness, hardly the norm for a tourist town, may be because Kanab is so remote. Unlike Orlando or Anaheim, where vacation-hungry families cram a month of sightseeing into three days, hurried tourists do not overwhelm the residents of Kanab. They are also a special breed of tourist. Visitors to Kanab have come a good distance to see and experience some of the most spectacular places on the planet. They want it at their pace, which is usually unhurried and deliberate.

Even today, this is a wild country, one of the largest expanses of wilderness in the lower forty-eight states. A hundred miles east of here are monoliths of crumbling rock brooding over a windswept desert. Under this lunar landscape is a vast amount of coal. So much coal, in fact, the ground has smoked for centuries from spontaneous combustion, and the cliff walls have turned scarlet from the heat. Known as the Kaiparowits Plateau, it contains 5 to 7 billion tons of coal, making it one of the nation's most valuable energy reserves. Were there to be a change in this wilderness, it would likely happen there. But in September 1996, the Kaiparowits and 1.7 million acres around it were set aside as a national monument.

Almost everyone in Kanab had wanted a proposed coal mine. It would have created hundreds of jobs and tax revenue. Then again, Kanab now has another wonderland, a wilderness this time, that Washington will open, promote, clean, and protect. And a road from Kanab leads to it.

47

Maybe America's Only Ant Hunter

Hurricane, Utah

If you ever visit Zion National Park, you will probably drive through Hurricane. Upwards of 2.6 million people do every year. In the summer, 4,000 to 5,000 cars pass through here every day, all headed for the park and its 400 parking spaces.

I was not one of those bound for Zion. I was just looking for the Ace Hardware store on the right side of Route 9 coming into town. There I would find the son-in-law of Afton Fawcett. At age seventy, Afton is probably America's only ant hunter. His son-in-law would certainly know where Afton lives.

So far so good. In the store, Afton's son-in-law was helping a lady select paint for her kitchen. She was confused—I couldn't blame her—by all the different names of paint colors that all look white.

"Is your wife's dad still in the ant business?" I asked, when my turn came.

"Oh, ya. He and my brother-in-law, too." He told me how to find the house. "I ought to know. I live next door." In fact, four of the six Fawcett children live in the same block Afton and his wife do, along with most of their twenty-five grandchildren.

I located Afton's house at the end of a wide street. There was plenty of room to park my motorhome. Wide streets are one thing you can depend on in Utah. Brigham Young, who brought his Mormon followers to Utah in 1847, drew the layout for towns in the state that is still followed today. Young insisted that streets be wide enough for a horse and buggy to turn around.

Afton's twenty-one-year-old daughter greets me at the front door. She called her dad from the basement, where he and his wife work much of the day. It's probably best described as their windowless sorting-assembling-packing-mailing room.

Waiting for Afton to climb the stairs, his daughter told me that she was just days away from going to Japan on an eighteen-month missionary assignment. A book she was reading said that Japan, not quite twice the size of Utah, has a population density of 863 people per square mile.

"How does that compare with Utah?" I asked, expecting a wild guess.

"Utah has 20 people per square mile as of the 1990 census," she replied, as if I had just asked for the time of day.

Afton appeared in the kitchen and invited me to take a seat at the table. Only after he knew me well enough, that is. Having lived his entire life in this small town, he knows everybody who knocks on his front door. I was an unknown, a curiosity as much as anything. Not that Afton did not trust me. I think by nature he trusts everybody. It was just that I was somebody new to get to know.

After hearing about my travels in the motorhome, he pushed aside a stack of mail and began telling me about the ant business. "This whole thing started over twenty-five years ago. We were collecting biological specimens for laboratories, which expanded into packaging different kinds of rocks and fossils for school science classes and the like. Then some big retail chains were looking for someone to supply ants to folks who bought ant farms in their stores," Afton explained.

I interrupted, "I remember buying one of those for my kids. It was a plastic box, about the size of book, right?"

Afton nodded. "Some are bigger. Anyway, packed with every farm is a coupon good for some ants. So they send that in, and I air-mail them a package of ants in a vial. We get flooded with orders at Christmas when kids get these ant farms and want them all up and running at the same time. Ants go out of here by the thousands. I even have to go out of town to find 'em on cold days."

Afton shuns publicity and has turned down attractive invitations from a long list of TV talk shows. He got up from his seat to pull a letter from some cookbooks on the kitchen counter. Postmarked 1991, it was from The Tonight Show. I suppose Afton was flattered and probably amazed that people find his work so interesting. But he told Johnny Carson no, and Jay Leno, too. And many more since.

As we talked, little kids passed silently through the kitchen, one at a time, headed for the basement. Afton paid no attention. One came up the stairs munching the remains of a cookie, which explained the stream of small-foot traffic.

After we toured the basement, it was time for an ant roundup. I was about to watch one of the few people in the world who does it.

We took off in Afton's pickup. During the summer, he does his collecting early in the morning when it is cool. During the winter, he gets what he needs in a couple of hours before noon. He collects only red harvester ants. They are the most active and plentiful ants here. If kept cool, they can survive without water for about three days, the normal shipping time.

Afton knows all the anthills around Hurricane. Each one, he said, shelters 5,000 to 50,000 ants. The first one we stopped at looked quiet to me.

On his hands and knees, Afton leaned forward and inserted a soda straw into the hole of the anthill. He then blew on the straw, which apparently created breezy turmoil in the ant colony. Out poured the ants. He rounded up a bunch, blowing them gently with his straw into a tin scoop. He took only a few before we moved to the next anthill. We returned home with maybe a thousand ants in mason jars.

With Afton's ant harvest in for the day, he now must ready for shipment some pressed wildflowers and tadpole-shrimp eggs. School science classes are the primary customers for those. So I headed into town. Afton pointed me toward city hall, where his son Clark has been city manager for the past thirteen years.

Clark answered the question that has been gnawing at me since I first heard of Hurricane.

"Hurricanes, as in weather, do not occur around here. What happened was, a gust of wind blew away the top of Erastus Snow's buggy, which was being lowered off the cliff behind me." Clark pointed over his shoulder. "That was in 1865, so who knows for sure what really happened. Anyway, Snow said something about the wind being a hurricane."

Since Snow was an important elder in the Mormon Church, what he said was considered noteworthy. Apparently, someone thought the "hurricane" comment was too. So the cliffs got the name, and the town picked it up later.

Curiously, people here don't pronounce the word like you and I do. They call it "Hurrican," with a soft a. In fact, many other words here sounded strange. A tongue-in-cheek glossary someone gave me was of help: People "pork cores in coreparts" and never put the "court before the harse," eat "cormel carn," shop at the "morket," or visit Disneyland in "Califarnia."

The accent is obvious and makes it easy to tell the natives from the newcomers. It is linked to the colorful potpourri of people who settled here. Among the first were cotton growers, who were bonafide Southerners. Add to these the Europeans—Swiss, Scandinavians and English—who settled nearby St. George. Then came the miners at Silver Reef, who added Chinese, Irish, Scottish, Cornish, and other languages and dialects. All melted into one culture, bringing forth local English that sounds like it was "barn in a born."

The center of town is the Pioneer Heritage Park and Museum, a first-class exhibit. It is typical of what I have seen so often in Utah. Steeped in the traditions of the Mormon

Church, people here demonstrate a deep respect for their pioneer ancestors.

The early explorers of the West—Lewis and Clark and others—have been given due credit for their brave accomplishments. Towns, rivers, even babies have been named after them. The pioneers were different. They were ordinary folks who left relative security to settle this country. They risked everything they had, including the lives of their families. Drawing the first map certainly took courage, but filling it in took much more. That's what the pioneers did.

In the park, I sat among flowers in the shade of a tall monument topped with the statue of a pioneer family. I wondered if future generations in Utah or anywhere else will create monuments to my generation and others of the twentieth century. Perhaps they already have, if war memorials are to be our monuments.

48

"Catfish" Charlie on Butch Cassidy

Leeds, Utah

"Butch Cassidy died right where you're settin'."

I squirmed in my chair. "No way!"

"Well...a log-cabin inn was here then." "Catfish" Charlie Scott rapped the table with his cigarette lighter, as if to pinpoint the spot.

"I saw on PBS one time, some anthropologists were looking for his bones in Bolivia."

"But they didn't find him, did they? Because he's not buried there. He's buried around here somewhere."

Were we playing poker, I would peg Charlie as a poor bluffer with a good hand. He had this smirk on his face. It's probably always there, like the straw hat that he never takes off. His wife tells him the hat is worn out and should be thrown away. But Charlie won't, saying it is just now becoming him.

I played into Charlie's hand. "I was told that he is buried up near Beaver, and that's less than a hundred miles from here."

"Could be. Butch was born in Beaver, you know."

It was too early for Charlie's dinner house to open, so we engaged in a good bit of uninterrupted talk. He left the table once to put potatoes in the oven. Catfish Charlie's, the only place around here to buy a meal, does not open until 4:00 p.m. He cooks the dinners. His daughter serves them. A few people order chicken tenders or buffalo shrimp, but everyone else eats deep-fried, farm-raised Mississippi catfish and hush puppies.

"Two houses down," Charlie continued, "is where the Sundance Kid was livin' at the time. His real name was Harry Loungabaugh, but he didn't use that here." Charlie pointed over his shoulder with an unlit cigarette he had been holding for a long while. "He used the name Hyman Beebee. People tell that he would pull a six-gun on kids if they got on his lawn."

"When was that?"

"Late thirties, I guess."

Since he moved to Leeds three years ago, Charlie has been researching Utah's best-known outlaws. Butch Cassidy and his gang, called the Wild Bunch, became infamous around the turn of the century. They robbed banks and trains in south-central Utah and elsewhere.

Charlie has an 1877 Colt 45 that he claims belonged to Kid Curry, one of the Wild Bunch. "I'm gunna have it in a nice glass case and put a price on it: $29,995. I know I ain't gunna sell it, but folks always want a price on things, especially things they can't have."

Although he has lived in Utah most of his fifty-five years, Charlie brought his accent with him from Oklahoma, where he grew up. Charlie says he "loves people to death," which may explain his immediate acceptance here in Leeds and his status as acting mayor.

Pointing to a row of fourteen cups hanging over the door, he started reciting the names of each owner. Charlie comes in every morning at 6:00, even Mondays when the restaurant is closed, to make coffee for them. They don't all show up, of course. Some live here only in the winter.

This town, like many others in the United States, took its name from somewhere else. A Mormon named it after Leeds, England, where he did missionary work.

There is one store here for everything. Cassidy's sells earrings, nachos, magazines, firewood, fishing tackle, and more. It rents videos and a Rug Doctor and provides coin-operated entertainment, principally pool and video games. Around noon on Mondays and Saturdays, owner Brant Jones hauls out a charcoal grill and makes buffalo burgers out front.

This was Saturday. In spite of the midsummer heat, Brant was out there in the sun, spatula in hand, watching cheese melt over buffalo. The aroma caught me as I left Charlie Scott's place.

Inside the store, Brant's spouse Tiffey tended the cash register and their two children, who were in a playpen. An enormous buffalo head hung on the back wall. Like the meat on the grill, the head came from Colorado. It carried a price of $1,200.

Rounding out the Yellow Pages of Leeds, if there are any, is Lisa's Corner Salon and a tidy RV park run by two hard-working ladies originally from Albuquerque, New Mexico. An art gallery is located in a house built by proprietor Joanne Thornton's great-grandfather. Add the U.S. Post Office, and that's it.

Leeds is a one-street town of trees and century-old homes, a few newer. Its ancestry is tied to nearby Silver Reef and Harrisburg. Both became ghost towns about the same time, but for different reasons. Their remains are now carefully preserved. Harrisburg is even fenced off and labeled. A new generation is moving in around them, bringing rock gardens, swimming pools, and the hum of air-conditioners.

49

Silver Oozed from the Rock

Harrisburg, Utah

A nearby newcomer, Interstate 15, runs through Utah from top to bottom. Its predecessor, Highway 91, passes through Leeds and goes on south three miles through the crumbling stone remains of Harrisburg. An RV resort has taken hold there. Respectful of their pioneer predecessors, developers have preserved the stone buildings of Harrisburg. Its old cemetery is restored, fenced in, and built around.

Harrisburg was never large nor prosperous. It peaked in 1868 with twenty-five families. Rocky ground gave them good material for building houses, but it was not much good for growing crops. Floods were all too common, as were swarms of grasshoppers. By the turn of the century, everybody had left.

Although Harrisburg did not last, a remarkable story that originated here is still alive. Every story out of the Old West seems to start with a freezing wind howling down the canyons. And that's how it was one winter night when an old silver prospector stopped for shelter at a farmhouse in Harrisburg. Invited in, a roaring fire drew him close to the sandstone fireplace. There he noticed drops of shining metal oozing from the rock. A closer look and he knew just what the metal was. Silver!

A ridge of rusty sandstone runs west of Harrisburg to the horizon. I assume the prospector got a fix on that ridge as the place where the fireplace builder got his rock. The fact that silver was there at all, geologists say, is a freak of nature. Silver in sandstone exists in only one other place in the world: Mannheim, Germany.

The facts of the 1868 silver discovery may be debatable, but the results are not. It changed lives, reshaped history, and created a town five miles north of Harrisburg called Silver Reef. By 1878, Silver Reef was the biggest town in southern Utah, with a population exceeding 1,500. The miners were largely Irish Catholics who poured into Silver Reef from mining towns in Nevada.

A curious situation developed in Silver Reef. An island of Catholics and some Protestants lived in a sea of Mormon pioneers and their descendants. The two groups got along in spite of significant differences in ideology and lifestyle. Together they made history when the Catholics celebrated high mass in the Mormon tabernacle in nearby St. George. Even the thirty-member Mormon choir participated, having practiced for two weeks from a single copy of music provided by the Catholic priest. On May 25, 1879, a congregation of 3,000 gathered in the tabernacle. Curious, respectful Mormons outnumbered the Catholics more than two to one.

After a few million dollars in silver were dug from the hills, and after a few shootings, lynchings, and hangings, the miners disappeared from Silver Reef as quickly as they had come. Stone walls and wood scaffolding, capsizing into the canyons, are all that remain, except for the bank and the Wells Fargo Express office. Said to be the only one remaining outside California, the Wells Fargo office is restored and is now a museum and gallery.

Comfortably plugged in at Harrisburg for the night, Rusty and I sat on the grass and watched rain clouds gather around the 10,000-foot peaks of the Pine Valley Mountains. Soft piano, as only Floyd Cramer could play it, drifted from the motorhome next door. The sun set and took with it the rust from the ridge of sandstone. It was a magnificent sight, just as it was a century ago.

Out there now is the interstate, which at twilight adds a contemporary magnificence of its own. Most people would not call it that, but it's a sight to be had only in America. Huge trailer trucks that yesterday may have been in a sandstorm in New Mexico or a downpour in Washington now roll through a sunset here in south-central Utah. Their drivers are just now turning on the lights that outline their huge rigs, adding to the visual awe of those mammoths of the American road.

50

Dixie Country

St. George, Utah

The next day, I followed Interstate 15 south a few miles to St. George, where the moving vans from Mayflower and United Van Lines run a constant shuttle service from southern California. This is just one popular destination on the flight-from-California list of the fed-up-and-over-fifty crowd.

The popular magazines that compile annual hit parades of cities of this country always rate St. George among the ten or twenty "best places to retire." Combine that with economics, and folks in Los Angeles do the logical thing. They sell their grossly appreciated homes there and recreate them here for half the price.

"Dixie Country," as this area of Utah is called, currently has about 4 percent of the state's population but 10 percent of its golf courses. There are no significant employers here, so wages are low. But the newcomers are not looking for jobs. The numbers most important to them are the crime rate, which is low, the current interest rate, and their tee times.

Dixie's year-round golf courses, spreading around red cliffs and lava-capped ridges, are all within a fifteen-minute drive of each other. And a golfer can play eighteen holes here in the afternoon, having spent the morning snow skiing at Brian Head or Elk Meadows.

Dixie got its nickname from its early settlers. Mormon pioneers came here in the winter of 1861, as directed by Brigham Young. Leaving their comfortable farms and homes in northern Utah, 309 families colonized this beautiful, albeit dusty, alkali flat. Many chosen for the task originally hailed from farms in Tennessee and Mississippi. And with good reason. Their mission was to raise cotton. The Civil War, just a few months old, had cut off sources of cotton to the North. Young's intention was to create a new supply. Their efforts met with only moderate success. With the end of the war and the railroad extending into Utah, cotton again became plentiful. The attempt to grow it here in Dixie ended. But the name stuck.

Brigham Young, the second president of the Mormon Church, was Dixie's first snowbird, at least the first prominent one. This was his winter retreat from Salt Lake City. His white-picket-fenced house gets top billing on the local tourist tour along with the Mormon temple, which ranks with the Eiffel Tower or the Hollywood sign as a dominant landmark.

Sun-seeking Northerners, golf bags in tow, flock here in big numbers to spend the winter. Even more briefly stop for a round of golf and then continue south into Arizona, where winter temperatures are warmer.

Eons before the first pioneers wandered this land, water and wind worked wonders. Alternating between inland seas and Sahara-like deserts, the elements created a great plateau of sandstone and limestone deposits thousands of feet thick. Over time, these gigantic sheets of rock buckled, folded, and uplifted. Massive sections were exposed to the forces of erosion, which sculpted the land into spectacular shapes and colors.

Utah's southern half has the most abundant and varied natural beauty of perhaps any state in the union. Until recent road improvements, it was the most remote region of the Lower Forty-eight.

I skirted St. George and headed north on Highway 18. About ten minutes after leaving the interstate, Rusty began racing around in the motorhome. She hopped on the couch and looked out the window for a few seconds. Then she hit the floor and disappeared somewhere in the back. A few seconds later, she reappeared and then did it all over again. This burst of energy had some unknown meaning, so I elected not to ignore it. I pulled off a road leading to Snow Canyon State Park.

Had it not been for Rusty's racing, I never would have seen this multicolored geological wonder. This canyon is a jumble of red-and-white Navajo sandstone with black lava flows pouring over its jagged cliffs. Greenery appears in the cracks and crevasses, softening the ruggedness of the canyon. Fine sand, the color and feel of ground paprika, supports hundreds of desert plants. The prevalent sagebrush has silver leaves as narrow as thread.

We wandered and explored. So beautiful, so close to the city, yet we saw few people. This must be paradise for a city dog like Rusty. It sure was for me.

51

A Monument to a Massacre

Mountain Meadows, Utah

A handbill stuck on the front of the Pine Valley General Store announced a rodeo tomorrow in Enterprise.

"Get off the mountain and back on the highway. Head north a few miles. You'll see it." In the store, a man standing with one leg and a crutch sketched the whereabouts of Enterprise, using his thumb as a pointer.

"Much of a rodeo?" I asked.

"Oh, yeah! Kids hereabouts are into rodeoing before they're into school. That one's an amateur rodeo, mostly local cowboys and youngsters. They got the same craziness as the pros, though, just no big pot to win." I felt a quick look-over. "And where might you be from?"

"On the coast, I guess. Utah is new to me."

"Then I'll bet ya don't know tomorrow here's a holiday, July 24. They always celebrate it in fine fashion down in Enterprise." He pointed his thumb again. "On the way, ya ought to stop at Mountain Meadows. That's where they had the big massacre, don't ya know?"

I told him I didn't know but certainly would stop.

Leaving a pleasantly cool elevation of 7,000 feet, my motorhome practically coasted out of the Pine Valley Mountains. I had second thoughts of forsaking brook fishing in an alpine campground for a hot, dusty, amateur rodeo.

Back on Highway 18 again, I remembered what he said about a massacre and wondered why I should know about it. So when the Mountain Meadows sign appeared, I pulled off onto a blacktop parking lot overlooking a tranquil, green valley that stretched for miles. I walked to an overlook. There stood a monument to the dead.

It happened in September 1857. Fifty-plus pioneer families from Arkansas were massacred in broad daylight. Only seventeen individuals, all children, survived. Mormon militiamen were the primary culprits. There are many accounts as to the reason of the massacre. The entire truth will probably never be known, because most of the documents and diaries of the participants were destroyed.

Although there were many investigations, no punishment was handed out for the crime until twenty years later. A Mormon elder, John Doyle Lee, who was almost like a son to Brigham Young, was returned to the site in 1877 and executed for leading the massacre.

The surviving children, ranging in age from nine months to six years, were taken into Mormon homes. But in September of 1859 Captain James Lynch, of the U.S. Army, took custody of all the children and returned them to their relatives in Arkansas.

There may have been an eighteenth child, a girl, who survived. It is not known what became of her. Some say she was later killed for talking too much. Others say that she was adopted by a childless Mormon family and lived out her life in Utah.

Although massacres are not uncommon in the history of the American West, what happened here almost a century and a half later definitely is. Descendants of both the perpetrators and the victims gathered here in September 1990 to bury their suspicions and anger. They dedicated the monument, a wall of Arkansas granite inscribed with the eighty-two known names of those who died at Mountain Meadows. The ages of the children, some as young as seven, are also etched in the white stone.

The memorial is located on a rise, where markers point out the route and campsite of the pioneers. It lies hidden from the highway. Were I not looking for it, I probably would not have stopped. I am glad to have seen this beautiful meadow with its remarkable memorial to tragedy, repentance, and forgiveness.

I think this place has human meaning that goes far beyond the picket-fenced residence in St. George or the monolithic temple there. Granted, I do not have the perspective of a Mormon. Yet, the initial and subsequent events that occurred here to me represent humanity at its very worst and its very best.

It takes no particular insight to understand why I find no reference to this historic spot in any of the local guides given to visitors to Utah. Maybe time will change that.

52

Pioneer Day

Enterprise, Utah

The tidy lawn of the town square is rimmed by huge shade trees, which were probably here in 1902 when this town was founded. I parked beneath one. Three stone buildings—all Mormon churches, each larger than the other—trace the growth of Enterprise.

I soon discovered that I was camped about dead center of a celebration that was to go on all the next day and into the night. July 24, 1847, is the day the Mormons arrived in Utah's Salt Lake Valley. Known as Pioneer Day, July 24 is now a state holiday. It is celebrated in Utah like none other.

It began at sunrise. A flatbed truck, with two loud speakers mounted on the cab, pulled up and parked ahead of me. Then, one by one, came the members of the Enterprise String Band. They climbed up a stepladder onto the truck bed and took seats down each side.

Sunlight now streaking through the trees, still a chill in the air, the band began playing and rolling through the streets of Enterprise as it has on this day for ninety years. In the beginning, the band played from a horse-drawn wagon. Now it's the same wagon pulled by a Ford truck.

"People used to sleep on their lawns so they could wake up to our music. Sometimes the lady of the house would bring out hot chocolate or lemonade," LaRae Pollock recalled. A resident of Enterprise for sixty-seven years, she has played guitar with the band since 1943. "We always play the same songs. We could learn new ones, I guess, but people would complain."

About seven-thirty the band turned the corner off Main Street playing "Camp Town Races." The truck pulled up to the curb and stopped. But the band kept on playing to the end of the song. Just for Rusty and me, I guess.

Rusty showed her appreciation with her usual tail wag that begins at her neck and works back. But Rusty was not altogether overjoyed when we all took off without her, walking across the square. That was where the aroma of frying bacon was coming from. This was no coach-class breakfast sizzling and popping on two, four-foot grills. About fifty people waited in line, carrying on as if at a family reunion.

Visiting around, I discovered that everyone was connected to Enterprise in some way. As usual, I was an oddity. In horse country, my white Reeboks stood out.

"Come on, eat with us!" somebody shouted.

The parade came next. Among the curios towed down Main Street was a weathered, wooden building: Utah's oldest tithing warehouse. "It was used in the olden days to store food," Mayor Merrill Staheli told me. "Someday it will be in the town park, when we get one."

The afternoon was busy with foot races and pie-eating contests for the kids. And there were a lot of kids. Obviously, this is no retirement community.

By late afternoon, dust was rising from the rodeo grounds at the edge of town. The rodeo arena was half circled with trucks, campers, and horse vans. Contestants pinned numbered cards to their shirts, having paid their two-dollar entry fees. Riders exercised their horses and looked over the competition. Although a tank truck was spraying water on the grounds, a haze still hung in the air.

Layne Gubler killed time honing his roping skills on a set of dummy horns. Repeatedly, he threw his lariat over the horns and yanked it taut. He never missed. "Like riding a bicycle," he said. "Ya never forget how."

In most of Utah and other Western states, learning rodeo skills is as much a part of the public school system as learning to play football or baseball. Of course, this sport requires a larger investment than a baseball glove, but there was no shortage of horses here. In most cases, one horse fits all. Incidentally, Enterprise High School has no football team, but it's a significant competitor in rodeo.

Steve and Janet Staheli's four children are all rodeo competitors, two of them since the age of five. "It's no more dangerous than whatever else kids do. It takes training and practice. With that comes confidence, for both the kids and the parents," Janet Staheli told me. "We go as a family to thirty-five or forty rodeos a year, all over Utah. We also farm. Sometimes I think that's secondary."

The next day, I stepped into the Big Valley Café on Main Street. Mule-deer and elk antlers covered the counter as did a year or two of dust that must blow in through the open door. Glass-eyed deer heads stared from the wall.

"If it's not a café, why don't you take down the café sign?" I asked Troy Truce Truman, who was in the back shop tacking a piece of green felt around the skull plate of a set of mounted antlers.

"People know my shop is in the café, so the sign makes it easy for them to find me," Troy replied, without looking up.

Deer-head mannequins and country-western music surrounded Troy. His radio cracked when the fluorescent light blinked.

"It started as a hobby, but about five years ago it became a business," he said. At thirty, he is a self-taught taxidermist and cabinetmaker.

"Around here a lot of us hunt. We enjoy the table fare and a trophy now and then. Still, you know, I see people coming up here to kill a mule deer just for a trophy." Although mounting trophies is his business, this was a sore point for

Troy. "It's becoming a rich man's hobby, a power thing. They aren't after meat. They won't even eat it."

Two women stopped by. They had found a freshly killed bobcat beside the highway and wanted to know if Troy might put it in his freezer. We looked at the dead animal spread out on the concrete stoop in front of the café. Troy identified it as a healthy female, not yet fully grown. Two young boys, skateboarding, came to stare but said nothing. I could feel the sadness among us.

Enterprise has a population of about 1,200 people and probably a third again as many horses. Some owners shoe their horses. Sandee Probst shoes the rest. A trim, thirty-one-year-old mother of two and former secretary from California, she is now the only farrier in town.

"I get kicked weekly, but it still beats being at a desk all day," Sandee admitted, brushing back her blond hair. "I work half a day, usually mornings. I take the kids and a cooler of soda pop with me in the truck. The rest of the day I'm a housewife."

Sandee, who is five-foot-two and weighs just 115 pounds, went to horseshoeing school in Porterville, California. "My class had thirteen men and three women, all bigger than me."

Before leaving town the next day, I visited the mayor. Brushing out a vacant lot with a backhoe, he was covered with dirt and sweat. I had enjoyed my time in Enterprise. I wanted to thank somebody, so I thanked him.

Heading north on Highway 18, all I could get on the radio was a talk show from somewhere far off. Gloomy people were rehashing the decay of American society. The host pontificated that nobody cares anymore. "We are all in a handbasket going nowhere good," he repeated several times.

I turned to Rusty, stretched out on her traveling seat. "That bozo has not a clue what America is about. He is like a shallow-rooted tree that can only report what goes on beneath its branches. Rooted, he can't see beyond his own shade, a dark spot of his own making."

Well, there are a bunch of fine folks out here sweating in the sun, brushing out the undergrowth, doing the best they can. What's more, they do it every day. If anybody wants to see just how well that works, how well that is turning out, come visit Enterprise sometime. Or thousands of towns like it in America. It's a great country. I love it.

Part V

Wyoming — Utah

53

Welcome to Wyoming

Evanston, Wyoming

Interstate 80 is called the Dwight D. Eisenhower Highway where it climbs over the Wasatch Mountains from Utah into Wyoming. At 6,680 feet, the mountain pass was used by the Pony Express in 1860 and 1861. Before that, it was the Mormon Trail.

Rusty and I are using it this Saturday as we enter America's least-populated state for the first time.

After passing several exits that offer "no services," we took one of three that offered Evanston. The gas stations at that exit all sported hand-lettered signs advertising clean restrooms. Were they having a contest?

Evanston is a tidy town of 11,000 people. The residential neighborhoods look like those idyllic scenes on Christmas cards, but without the snow. I passed white steeples and houses of red brick. Lawns and gardens showed loving care by those who make the most of a three-month summer.

I parked across the street from the Joss House, a replica of a Chinese sacred temple. It's now a museum. Still, it's the last thing I expected to find. Up here, the bucking bronco and the buffalo vie for the official state symbol. But Evanston is a railroad town. Of course, mostly Chinese labor built the railroads across the West.

I walked to the restored Union Pacific Depot. With heavy transcontinental passenger traffic, this was a busy train station from the day it was built in 1900. The traffic slowed a good thirty years ago. Thankfully, the ambiance is still here. The depot has two waiting rooms. The one for women and children once had a beautiful fireplace. The other, for the men, once had a spittoon and a potbellied stove. But someone, in the name of "improvement," took those out years ago.

Across an attractive brick walkway lined with well-tended flower boxes is a Carnegie library. Steelman Andrew Carnegie built 1,679 public libraries in communities across the United States between 1889 and 1923.

Well into my walk around town, it started to rain. Wyoming raindrops are the biggest I have ever seen. It takes only a few, I quickly discovered, to get a person seriously wet. I ducked and ran for the closest cover.

It turned out to be a rambling wooden porch draped with colored lights. It overflowed with a wedding party that had been celebrating for probably as long as I had been in Wyoming. Shaking off the rain, I was handed an opened bottle of beer with a label I had never seen before. I got acquainted with the groomsmen instantly. What a beautiful bunch! They were dressed in traditional black formal garb from neck to waist. The rest was Levis, boots, and handsome black cowboy hats.

Knowing that I had to get my motorhome somewhere for the night, I pushed aside glasses of champagne offered by these beautiful folks I didn't even know. In shorts and Reeboks, I was a curious party crasher, for sure. Still, I have never received a warmer, more sincere welcome my first day anywhere. Wyoming and I were off to a great start.

54

A Subterranean City

Lyman, Wyoming

I drove through a meadow of midsummer green and up a little bluff that displayed an enormous L of white rocks. Instantly, I was in downtown Lyman. With a population of 1,900, it's supposedly the biggest town in Bridger Valley. I am taking their word for it today.

Nothing moved on Main Street. Nor is there a sign that anything ever has. Six lanes wide, there's not so much as a pickup truck left in front of John's Bar and Lounge from last night. Even the air doesn't move. Flags hang like plywood from every street-side light pole.

"Rusty, something is about to happen here that everyone knows about but me, like a high-noon shoot-out in the middle of Main Street."

Rusty just stared at me from the other seat. I dropped the subject.

Then I passed the Mormon church with its perfect lawn. The parking lot was full, pickups mostly. What a relief! Things are just as they should be on a Sunday morning in a mostly Mormon town.

Halfway down Main Street, I saw other signs of life at the 7-Eleven. I parked in front. Inside Tami Chandler worked the

levers of a machine coated with frost, streaming orange Slurpee into a foot-high container. Watching the process—it took
a while—was a hefty lady with a tattoo on her shoulder.

"Can one person drink all that?" I asked as Tami handed
the Slurpee to the woman.

Her wide face, a total grin, turned toward me. I noted a
second tattoo, a rose, partially hidden by the top of her
low-cut dress.

"On a hot day they go down like nothin'." She held up
the family-size Slurpee so I could get a better look. "See, that
ain't much."

I wanted to ask about the rose tattoo but didn't dare. I
knew that, too, would be offered up for a better look.

Tami's husband Bruce sat behind the counter. He is a
trona miner. When Tami works, on weekends, Bruce keeps
her company.

Trona mining is the biggest industry in southwest Wyoming, which has the world's largest mine. Trona is the natural
source of soda ash used in the manufacture of glass, baking
soda, soap and detergents, sugar, soda pop, paper, even junk
foods. The five trona mines, forty miles east of the Bridger
Valley, reportedly produce 90 percent of the soda ash used in
the United States and 25 percent of the world's supply.

The mine of the FMC Corporation, the largest but typical
of the others, is a subterranean city. It has about 2,000 miles
of underground "streets," more than the city of San Francisco.
They are wide enough for two-way vehicle traffic and go
down as deep as 3,000 feet.

The mines operate day and night. Pay is good. The miners even have a non-contract fringe benefit. Because their
clothes pick up so much soda ash on the job, they don't have
to add soap when they wash them.

Rusty and I spent the night at the KOA Campground near
Lyman. Clark Anderson owns it. As if a father of eleven
doesn't already have enough to occupy his time, Clark is
running for county supervisor. He will win. He is a likable
guy. He jokes that the real winner may get the fewest votes.

"Then he won't have to do all that county business," Clark jokes.

55

Oregon Trail Trading Post

Fort Bridger, Wyoming

The next day, I accepted Clark's offer to use his car to visit Fort Bridger. Rusty stayed with the motorhome. Since Clark had a couple of friendly dogs, Rusty preferred it that way.

About fifteen miles from Lyman, Fort Bridger is a state historic site. Restored and reconstructed in fine and authentic detail, it recreates several layers of U.S. history beginning in 1843, when mountain man Jim Bridger and a partner built a trading post here. Fort Bridger was first an important supply point on the Oregon Trail, a 2,170-mile route that nearly half a million emigrants used to cross the better part of the continent. Through here passed the greatest human migration in history.

The Mormon Trail traced the Oregon Trail east of Fort Bridger, but it split here and proceeded into the Salt Lake Valley. By 1850, Jim Bridger was gone. The Mormons ran the trading post.

When the U.S. Army ran the Mormons out in 1858, Fort Bridger became a military outpost.

With the military came Judge William Carter. He had the concession to sell whatever the military commissary did not, everything from eyeglasses to whiskey. The customers of his Post Trader's Store were emigrants, Indians, railroad builders, settlers, and soldiers. Carter died a wealthy man in 1891. His descendants still live around here. I met one of them.

"When I'm alone in the store, surrounded by things of the Carter family, I think about them. It is a warm feeling to still be a part of it, even a hundred years later." At age twenty, Amber Aimone is a fort docent. The docents all wear period clothes and carry the title of "living historians." Her presence gives personal credibility to an important period of Fort Bridger's existence. Judge Carter was her great-uncle.

On the way back to the campground, I stopped at Urie Crossroads for a buffalo burger. The only other customer in the restaurant was a local lady who knew about buffalo.

"Oh, buffalo meat is leaner," she said. "That's why they say it is better for you than beef. I suspect tourists try it just because it's different. You're a tourist, right? You're eating it."

"Well, I'm eating it, but mostly because I'm hungry."

"So?" She paused, "What do you think?

"I think once it's in a hamburger bun and covered with ketchup, I can't tell the difference."

"The difference is, it costs more."

She lives near Fort Bridger, not far from Amber Aimone. "There's a lot of Aimones on the old county road where I live. So many, in fact, they are going to name the road after them. It was not a simple decision," she explained. "They came out from the county office and counted the Aimones and the Taylors who also live along there. It took two days, with long coffee breaks. I watched them. They found more Aimones than Taylors, I guess. Naming a road by counting noses. That's got to be the most stupid way to spend county money."

"What if they had named it for you?"

"Oh, that's different. Money well spent!" she laughed.

56

Greatest Pioneer Movement in History

South Pass, Wyoming

Four months ago, I sat at a lone campsite in the desert with an inspiring lady named Emmy. Spring flowers had made that southern California desert into a mosaic of yellow and blue. Color was everywhere that day. Talking mostly about her travels, Emmy asked me if I had seen the ruts left by the wagons on the Oregon Trail. I told her that I had not. "You will," Emmy assured me. "The roads you travel will lead you right to them."

Emmy was right.

"Indelible records," they call them up here, the tracks that steel-rimmed wagon wheels made 150 years ago. They show themselves as ruts and shallow swales in the grasslands of the prairie and the open desert, which is scattered with the same sagebrush and greasewood that has grown here for centuries. To the east, in mounds of sandstone around Guernsey, Wyoming, they are cut so deep in solid rock they defy logic. Obviously not created by nature, I could believe them being chipped out with a jackhammer and maybe a little dynamite. But wagon wheels? Even a million of them? It seems impossible.

Having left Lyman this morning, I headed eastbound on Highway 28 out of Farson. The highway roughly parallels the Oregon Trail as far as South Pass, a distance of forty miles.

The Oregon Trail enters Wyoming from Nebraska eighty miles north of Cheyenne and follows the Platte River west as far as it goes across the state. Southwest of Casper, it picks up the Sweetwater River and tracks it to the Continental Divide at South Pass. Then it heads southwest toward Utah, but turns north just short of the state line at Fort Bridger and goes on into Idaho.

Actually, it is three trails in one through here: the Oregon, Mormon, and California Trails. Whatever an emigrant's destination west of the Rockies—except for the far Southwest—there was only one way over those mountains. That was South Pass, with its easy gradients for wagons. This wide saddle across the Continental Divide made this massive migration possible. Were it not for the thousands of Americans who crossed through South Pass in the mid-1800s, the United States would very likely have a different shape today.

This was an epic migration. Half a million people walked this trail. Walked is certainly the word. Little kids, pregnant women, everybody. Some did it barefoot. Although most of them traveled in small groups of family and friends, the entire trail was a rolling community during the summer days between 1847 and 1855.

By 1850, with the California gold rush at its peak, the trail became one long train of wagons and livestock that moved all day. A checkpoint traffic counter probably would have seen 50,000 wagons during a thirty-day period. Diaries of those who made the trek from the Missouri River to what is now Oregon tell of a string of wagons as far as they could see. The trail was easy to follow. No wagon master was needed. You just had to keep from eating the dust of the guy ahead.

I left the highway east of the Continental Divide, dropping into a little valley and a long-abandoned mining town called South Pass City. The original town is well preserved and operated by the state as a historic site.

Ironically, thousands stampeded right by here, inflamed with California gold fever in the wake of the gold strike at Sutters Mill in 1848. Little did they know that gold would be discovered right here in 1867, creating boomtowns like South Pass City. The guys who discovered this gold were a bunch of disappointed prospectors returning home empty-handed from California.

But I was not here to talk gold. Luckily, I ran into Candy Moulton, a really neat lady who has lived all her forty-something years in Encampment, Wyoming. Candy is a fine journalist and a true Wyoming historian. She was here alone, taking pictures. Candy knows more about the Oregon Trail than most of us know about the streets we live on. She has written books about it and has crossed much of it over the past five years on vintage wagon trains.

"I don't do it as the pioneers did," Candy said. "For the most part, I ride in the wagon. They walked. I wear Wranglers and occasionally a skirt. Pioneer women always wore dresses that tangled and snagged in the brush along the trail. Yet I have been fortunate to see the land exactly as they saw it."

Candy and I found a shaded bench in front of the restored South Pass Hotel. We sat where the stagecoach once stopped. The hotel was built in 1868, long after the Oregon Trail was displaced by the railroad.

The smell of brewing coffee drifted our way from inside the wooden building.

"They really go for realism here."

Candy laughed. "You think it's just for effect, some aroma-making machine created by Hollywood?"

Actually, a group of ladies was setting up inside to sell homemade pies, to raise money to restore the site. The pies were ready, but not the coffee, I discovered.

Candy continued: "Sometimes it's necessary to mentally erase highways, roads, and power lines. But at other times, and particularly in sections of central and western Wyoming, that's not necessary. The covered wagon bumps over a landscape little changed, where the only road is the trail itself.

Those are the places where the true trail experience happens, where the threads of the frontier have not unraveled.

"The greatest thrills are when something happens on the trail which might have happened exactly the same way, and in the same place 150 years ago. Like a wagon tipping over halfway up a steep hill, sleeping in a tent in the rain and feeling the water seep through your sleeping bag, slapping mosquitoes, dodging a rattlesnake, fighting wind, taking care of blisters on your feet, or waking up to find the temperature so low, the water is frozen in the bucket. That's all part of it."

A couple of pie shoppers asked us for directions. We sent them inside the hotel.

"Enough of this busy city life," Candy said, "let's go." We hopped in her blue Subaru Outback and headed for South Pass. There we would find the actual Oregon Trail and the geographic marvel that made it possible.

At South Pass, the terrain was as gentle as a prairie. It was hard to believe that we were at 7,550 feet, standing at the pinnacle, the backbone of the North American continent.

The trail is obvious here. Equally obvious is how it was made. It is not a straight line, as Candy or I would create it, driving a vehicle across the land. The oxen pulling the wagons followed paths of least resistance. They stepped around things, not over them. Consequently, the trail is crooked, with no consistency as it wanders from side to side. We drove on it for a ways, long enough for me to appreciate that those who walked it had the right idea.

On the way back to South Pass City, I asked Candy about Indian attacks along the trail. She said that most emigrants never saw an Indian. Time and geography were their enemies, not Indians.

"When I hear or read about how the trail changed the West by pushing Indians from their lands, I am reminded that change is a part of life," Candy reflected. "The very tribes that were displaced by the trail had earlier displaced other tribes. Even today, that continues.

"When they protest grazing or timber sales, today's environmental activists are affecting people whose fathers and grandfathers claimed this territory and pioneered the West. The ranchers of recent generations are being moved off the land just as surely as the Indians of the mid-1850s were. In both cases, the movement was and is unfair and life-changing. It happened, or is happening, because someone believes he is right, which by a darn sight doesn't make it so."

57

The Beaver Hat

Pinedale, Wyoming

Who would have thought the whims of fashion—men's fashion at that—played a major role in the opening of the American West? That's what they say in Pinedale. Up here, high in the Wyoming Rockies at the headwaters of the Green River, they also say, "No more!" The West has opened far enough.

In the mid-1820s, mountain men wandered the outer and upper reaches of the West. Here, the less adventuresome drew the line. Only the skilled survivors went up these mountains. Or, more correctly, only they came down. Mountain men were a loose band of trappers and fur traders. Here they sought to fill the world's insatiable appetite for beaver pelts. Among the boulevard dandies of New York, Paris, and London and smartly uniformed armies, the beaver hat ruled supreme. Bold loners of the frontier, mountain men preceded the missionaries, the cattlemen, the wagon masters, and the settlers. Not only did they open much of the Rocky Mountain West, they also planted American's firm claim to it. Eventually, a nation followed their solitary pathways to the western sea.

Still they come, almost two centuries later. They travel on dual-lane highways that are marked where to camp, sleep, eat, refuel, and where to turn back in a winter snowstorm. Their reasons for coming are as plentiful as their numbers. With them come dreamed-of opportunities and nightmarish challenges for a small town like Pinedale.

"When we started the store in 1947, our customers were ranchers, our friends. Now they are tourists that pass through with the summer. That's OK, I guess, but where are we going from here?" Caryn Murdock Bing runs the Cowboy Shop. It smells of leather and stocks everything for the working and nonworking cowboy, plus anything wearable called Western.

She taught school in Wyoming for forty-three years. Her first school—one room, grades one through eight—was the one she loved the most. It was made of logs. "The kids and I scrubbed the wood floor. In the winter, which was most of the year, the kids would break a hole in the ice to get the water, then haul it up from the river."

Like others I met in Pinedale, population 1,200, Caryn loves her hometown. Rolling ranch land to the south changes dramatically at the town limits. From here north is the rugged Bridger-Teton National Forest, the second largest in the United States outside Alaska. Some of its glacial lakes have granite bottoms deeper than 600 feet. Fifteen miles from town is Gannett Peak. At 13,804 feet, it's the highest in Wyoming.

At an elevation of 7,175 feet, Pinedale's winter days are hard and short and extend for eight months. Yet summers are gorgeous. Those summers, combined with extraordinary natural beauty, draw millions of people every year to Wyoming, the nation's ninth largest state but the least populated. It's the home of Grand Teton and Yellowstone National Parks, both a few hours' drive from here.

Pinedale's dilemma is as old as progress. How does a small town stay small when outsiders and newcomers want more from it? It's not like they don't have the money to pay for it. They do. Some here think too much.

"For a while here, if a rancher mumbled something about selling his spread, the next day he had an offer on it from

California or somewhere. What private land there is around here, I think, is passing into fewer and fewer hands," a clerk in the Coast to Coast Hardware told me. "And many don't live here but a few months of the year. Then they want a resident hunting license and get mad because I can't sell them one."

Jill Straley runs a neat bookstore on Main Street. She explains it this way: "Absentee owners don't give back to the community. They might shop here, but there is more to being part of a place than buying groceries and renting videos."

I walked across the town's grassy park to Pine Creek. Four boys were totally focused on what swims in it. What may or may not be happening elsewhere in Pinedale, or on the planet for that matter, was of no interest or concern to them. This was summer. In six weeks, it will be gone. Two were fishing with worms on hooks and two with sticks with forks attached.

"Got to be careful spearing bullheads," one of the fork-fishermen said. He stood ankle-deep in rushing water that would complement a Sparkletts Water commercial. "If ya spear your foot, that hurts."

"Ever happen?" I asked.

"No, but my brother poked his toe. Said it hurt so much he lost the fish."

I have always thought of Wyoming as a man's country, but women have a big influence here. Wyoming was the first state to give women the right to vote. It was also the first to elect a woman as governor. The mayor of Pinedale is a woman, as are two of the four people on the city council.

Women run many businesses here, like the Sublette Stage, a taxi-shuttle service. At age thirty-three, Kathy McCarty started it three years ago, with nothing more bankable than an idea.

Kathy grew up in the 1960s on a ranch near here. She rode a snowmobile to where she caught the school bus. Her family had no telephone, no TV. Her study-light was a Coleman lantern. To say they had no running water tells only half the story. They hauled it in and hauled it out again.

I dropped by Kathy's house, which is also her office. Her four children, ages six and less, had just finished lunch. She cleared the table and poured us coffee. I walked to the back door, which opened onto an enormous pile of firewood.

"What you see is our heat for the next nine months. I'll split, stack, and cover that wood before the first freeze."

Kathy has three vehicles and three on-call drivers, including her mother, when she is in town. They run to the area guest ranches and to the airports in Rock Springs or Jackson, one to two hours away. Backpackers are a growing group of customers. Kathy takes them to a trailhead, then picks them up a day or two later when they come out.

Like many here, Kathy's business is seasonal. What it takes to support her family for twelve months she has to make in four. Once the snow flies, it's all over until next year.

One woman here everyone speaks of as a local celebrity. She is Madge Funk. Madge grew up in La Cross, Wisconsin and went to college in Minnesota. She came to Wyoming in the mid-1920s.

"As a young girl, I loved the wonderful western novels by Zane Grey. They ran in Country Gentleman magazine. It came in the mail once a week, always at noon. My father used to say, 'Can't you set it aside long enough to eat lunch?'

"I came to Wyoming at the urging of a school friend. Here I met a man Zane Grey wrote about, Jack Funk. And we got married. Isn't that something?" Madge's voice rose half an octave, as if, after all these years, she still couldn't believe it.

"Which book?" I asked.

"Man of the Forest." She handed me a copy, which I quickly noticed had been handed around many times. "That's Jack Funk," she said, pointing to a framed photo, one in a cluster of many.

For decades, Madge has lived in the same log house, shaded by a big cottonwood tree and flanked by tidy stacks of firewood. In the winter, they are the only source of heat for her and Rusty. She has had many dogs, all named Rusty.

I told her about my Rusty and that I named her after my first dog, although she is mostly black.

Her response I will always remember. She looked me squarely in the eye and said, "I am so very glad to meet you."

We talked about the mountain men. She said they lasted only sixteen years here. Then the silkworm replaced the beaver. The silk hat came into fashion, the beaver hat went out. By 1840, the mountain man was history. The beaver was almost extinct.

"Lucky for him, too," Madge said. "They took about 100,000 pelts out of here."

58

Ranch Girls Aren't Prissy

Sublette County Fair, Wyoming

Horses trotting out tight figure eights on parched ground made the hot air a dusty haze. I tried to park up-wind of it, but there was no such place.

This is the fair of Sublette County, the third least-populated county in the nation's least-populated state. For that reason alone, I had to stop.

The air is permeated with the smell of fresh straw and manure, not that of diesel exhaust from noisy engines powering a Loop-to-Loop or a Ferris wheel. No gaudy sideshows. No cotton candy. No pushy crowds. This is a back-to-basics county fair.

An historic marker just beyond the fairground fence proclaimed this spot as part of the Lander Cutoff from the Oregon Trail. Those who chose this grueling shortcut crossed a barren, arid stretch of Wyoming, where for fifty miles there was no water and little grass. They saved eighty-five miles of travel and gained a week. They also forfeited the chance to rest and resupply at Fort Bridger.

Leaving Pinedale this morning, I had come south down U.S. 189, over much the same type of country. The morning had been chilly, but now it was hot.

The Green River flows by here, heading south to join the Colorado. A few days ago, it was last winter's snow. It came from high in the Bridger-Teton National Forest. I could only guess, as sweat ran down my back, what seeing that river meant to those emigrants and their livestock.

What happened here 150 years ago had nothing to do with what was happening here today. Surrounding me were ranch animals and the young kids who care for them, the best of both. Yesterday were the rabbit and poultry judging, 4-H dog show, cookout, and free concert by the Cowpatsys. I had already missed the floriculture and vegetable judging today, but I am just in time for the Open Angus Steer Show.

I watched kids vacuum, clip, and brush their steers, whose lustrous, black hides were like silk. Docile as kittens, grooming was not new to these animals. The final touch was a glue, sprayed on the tail. The long tail hairs, which normally swish flies, were curled back on themselves. The tail ended up looking fluffy like a pom-pom. Some were then protected in a plastic bag. The primping seemed better suited for a toy poodle than a 1,200-pound animal that nature meant to be a bull.

Taylor Bardin gave her handsome steer a finishing spit of glue and left to dress herself for the show. Incidentally, there is a dress code for showing animals in the West, maybe everywhere: no ball caps, ever.

I watched the pom-pom on Taylor's steer go up in the air. He then did what cattle do naturally and quite often. Following which, he laid down, front legs first. Then the rest of him settled with a splat.

Taylor returned, looking like a western doll, wearing a belt buckle as big as a donut. She stopped dead, glaring for the longest time at her steer in his messy midday siesta. She said nothing. Her boot, however, made what might be a permanent dent in a future rump roast. But it got him on his feet.

"Can you hose it off?" I asked.

"No," Taylor said, simply grabbing some towels to wipe down his hindquarter. The pom-pom survived.

"Ranch girls aren't prissy," a lady beside me said. "They do what they have to do." The lady was cleaning white foam from the mouth of her family's steer. He was massive.

My expression must have asked the next question, for she answered it. "He drools because he's nervous. After a few days at home, when the adrenaline is flushed out of his system, he'll be fine. Then he goes to the butcher." She said this as if talking about someone else's animal, while giving hers a loving pat. Frankly, I flinched.

"The other animals here will be butchered probably Monday or Tuesday. Steer meat is not as good when charged with adrenaline. So they are the only animals that go back to familiar surroundings for a week or so to mellow out."

I couldn't believe this. She told me every animal would be sold at auction on Sunday, the last day of the fair. The sale price includes delivery to the buyer's choice of slaughterhouse.

"You mean these kids raise these beautiful animals all year, show them here, maybe they win them a prize, and then they send them off to be slaughtered?"

"That's what it's all about. Rural kids are very realistic. They see the animal world as a continuing cycle. It's always going to end the same way, and they accept that. This steer is part of a cash crop. What this big guy brings on Sunday will go into my son's college fund."

"Don't you get attached to one once in a while?"

"Sure, we get attached. They all have personalities, but they are not pets. It helps to give them names like 'Beefsteak' and 'Rib Eye.' That puts the focus in the right place, I think.

"Kids out here take responsibility at an early age. Ranch life demands it. Maybe they grow up quicker than city kids do. I'm not saying it's good or bad, it's just the way it is. They live close to the land, closer to God, maybe."

We watched as her son stuffed a big comb in the back pocket of his jeans. "And they also learn showmanship," she added, laughing. "If a judge touches the steer, the hand-print is instantly combed out."

I walked to the swine shed, where the hogs were all asleep. No adrenaline rush there.

In the crafts building, I waited in line to buy bread and sample brownies. A sign advertised the annual Lions Club spaghetti dinner tonight. Behind me someone said, "The person who usually makes the spaghetti sauce can't do it this year, so it could be pretty good."

59

J.C. Penney Mother Store

Kemmerer, Wyoming

A dog-eared sign, stuck on the door, read "Back in 15 Minutes." Starting when? How long has it been here? This was no hastily scribbled note by a conscientious store owner called out unexpectedly. That's forgivable. This hand-lettered sign showed age and heavy use. Guess you can get away with that in a small town, where you can survive with no competition.

Since the store was dark, fifteen minutes could mean anything, maybe even tomorrow. By then, I could be somewhere else.

I crossed the street to a shady bench in the town square, which is a grassy triangle here in Kemmerer. Most of the retail business in town happens on two of its sides.

The vehicles around the square confirmed a notion I have had since entering the state. Should Wyoming ever need a symbol to rival the cowboy on a bucking bronco, which appears on every license plate, or the bison, which decorates the state flag, it has one in the pickup truck. Men and women. Young and old. If they drive anything here, it is a truck of some sort, most often a pickup.

Another consistency: all these pickups are American made. A while back, there was a Nissan pickup around town. The retired gent who owned it was hounded unmercifully by his lunch buddies at the senior center. They kidded him that he should be made to go to Japan to get his Social Security check.

From my bench in the square, now getting warm in the sun, I counted two cars. They passed on Pine Street, which is also U.S. 189. I didn't count them in my bench survey because they had out-of-state license plates.

Big beneficiaries of this pickup society are dogs, big ones especially. They hop in the trucks, even with muddy feet, and visit the town square to bark and be barked at. I saw many that were doing just that. I bet dogs live happy lives in Wyoming. I felt sorry that I left Rusty with the motorhome. She would have had fun in the town square.

On the corner of Pine, across from the square, is the J.C. Penney Store. This is not just any J.C. Penney Store, one of 1,300 outlets in malls and on main streets across the country. This is the J.C. Penney Company Mother Store, "Founded in 1902," so the sign says that spreads across its front.

Penney named his original store the Golden Rule after the biblical rule that he lived by. That store has been torn down. So they can't honestly hang a sign on this one calling it the original. But "Mother Store" is good enough. It makes the point: James Cash Penney started here in Kemmerer.

The local banker warned Penney and his two partners that a cash-only store could not make it here. Three others had tried and failed. They could not compete with the mining company's store that offered credit and accepted mining-company script, cautioned the banker.

Penney did not take the banker's advice but he took his money, $1,500.00, and added $500.00 of his own. At age twenty-six, he was an instant success in the dry-goods and clothing business. Considering suspenders sold for 5 cents and ladies' satin petticoats could be had for 29 cents, this put his first-day sales in perspective. He closed with an impressive $466.59, and that in a town of just 1,000 people!

Farther down the square, near the point of the triangle, is the white-picket-fenced house of the Penney family. This is the original house, but it's not in its original location. In the 1980s, they moved it to make it more accessible to summer visitors like me. (Nobody visits here in the winter.) If they can move the house, the least I can do is walk over for a closer look.

Shirley Kindschuh was sweeping the porch. "Someone lived in it up 'til the seventies, even though it has no indoor plumbing," Shirley said, as we walked from one small room to another and up and down some tight stairs.

Completing the tour, Shirley offered me a place to sit in Penney's parlor: the love seat. We talked about why she liked Kemmerer. Fishing. Deer hunting. Camping. Also, what she called, "snow machining"—apparently a Wyoming word for what others call "snow mobiling."

She had to leave about the time I realized that Penney's love seat is stuffed with something as comfortable as crumpled cardboard. If it's a Penney's original, I don't think Penney or anyone else sat on it much.

I wanted to visit Kemmerer's town hall until I learned that it was in another town. It's in Frontier, a community just up the road. Kemmerer got a good deal on a building in Frontier. Having the town hall out of town was one thing, but having it in another town rubbed civic pride a little raw. So Kemmerer annexed a corridor that technically puts the town hall within the town limits. It also puts Frontier's post office in Kemmerer.

I was curious to see how this is working out, but Frontier is too far to walk. I opted for the Senior Friendship Center. It's next to the Penney house.

Entering this small-town senior center during lunch stopped everything. My slamming the door didn't help. Forks, spoons, napkins, cups, even heads and eyes, everything froze as in a photograph. They didn't just stare. They gawked. For an instant, I could read the cartoonist's balloons over every gray head: Who is this guy, and why is he late for lunch? I wanted to yell, "I'm not here for lunch!" But a pretty lady in a flowered apron put a tray in my hands and led me to the fried chicken, mashed potatoes, Kool-Aid, and salad. I was glad I didn't yell anything about lunch.

I found a seat across from Ben Brown. Ben and his late wife were ranchers here for many years. Even at age eighty-seven, he remembers those days well. "But they roll by so fast now, it's hard to keep track of dates," he admitted.

"I think it was in the twenties," Ben recalled, "or maybe the thirties." Anyway, whenever Prohibition was. Kemmerer was where the really good shine came from. They called it 'Kemmerer Moon.' It kicked like a bull. You could get it anyplace in Wyoming, Montana, Colorado, even in Chicago. Back there it was Al Capone's favorite drink."

The fellow sitting next to Ben interrupted. "You know the saying 'I'd kill for it'? Well, it was Al Capone who said that, and he was talking about Kemmerer hooch."

Ben gave him a side-glance and continued. "Corn sugar came here by the trainload. So did the big whiskey vats made somewhere back east. The revenuers would wheel in here, raid a few stills, and bust things up. One time they split open 15,000 gallons of prime, uncut shine. There were some tears shed that night, I tell ya. Another thing, unemployment was unheard of. Anybody who wanted a job could be a driver.

"The sheriff put guys in jail now and then, but he let them out a couple of times a day to go home to stir their mash. He didn't want it to spoil, either. The used-up mash, they would feed to the animals. It was good for 'em. Nothing funnier than a drunk chicken, except maybe a plastered pig."

We finished off the Kool-Aid and said our good-byes. Ben stepped into the other room to play pool.

I had that mournful feeling again, that certainty of the roads I travel. Good-byes are frequent. Most always, they are permanent.

Heading back to the Riverside RV Park, I walked over a bridge, under which runs the Hams Fork River and the tracks of the Union Pacific Railroad. A path runs off the end of the bridge, by a riverside bird sanctuary, and to a road that took me home.

Rusty seemed only moderately interested in my return. She looked exhausted. Before I left, two neighborhood kids asked me if they could take her for a walk while I was in town. I told them they could. I think they walked her while they rode their bikes.

This RV park shows years of hands-on care, obviously a family effort. It is tidy and very comfortable, but has no amenities, not even showers. Shower stalls are here, but a sign said that they did not work. Frankly, I didn't believe it. It appeared that the likable couple who run the park were appropriately enjoying the short summer here with their eleven-year-old grandson. After many years of cleaning up after strangers, they were probably sick of it.

There are times—and a Wyoming summer is a good one—to say the hell with it and hang up an Out of Order sign. But never a sign that reads Back in 15 Minutes!

60

Inside the Temple

Manti, Utah

Gray and hard, the morning light reminded me of old concrete. It moved on the dirty sky with as much agility. Being held hostage by a cold rain was the good news. The bad news was it would soon turn to an even colder snow.

Inside my motorhome, though, it was as warm as I wanted it. I had plenty of coffee. The TV worked on four channels. I was plugged into Yogi Bear's Jellystone Park in Manti, Utah, population 2,200, elevation 5,500 feet. This was the only RV park in town, and a really nice one. Again, that was the good news. The bad news was, I was the only one in it, and Yogi Bear would shut down for the winter in another couple of days.

Rusty liked it because she had the run of the place. Rollicking in the fallen leaves was a new experience for her. I watched her, wondering what she will think tomorrow if the leaves are all under snow, which would be another first for her.

Yesterday, under low clouds, their serrated edges clinging to the mountains of the Manti-La Sal National Forest, I drove through the middle of Utah on U.S. 89. The sun peeked out now and then, like the opening eye of a doped patient. The brief beam showed pine trees covered with fresh snow high in the mountains.

Manti's distinguished landmark, built over a century ago, is no less prominent or magnificent than the castles of Europe. It overlooks—no, dominates—the Santepe Valley from a promontory higher than the town's tallest trees. Built of white oolite limestone, the Manti Mormon Temple rises to 179 feet at its highest point, its elegant east tower.

I saw it from five miles out. On a clear night, they say, it is visible at distances four times that. It is awash in electric light from dusk to dawn. With that, this Mormon temple and the six others in Utah part comparison with the castles of Europe. Castles settle for moonlight.

Like all towns in Utah—Salt Lake City included—Manti is laid out like a checkerboard. All corners are square. Streets run to the four points of the compass. There is always a ground zero, usually at Main and Center Streets, from which street numbers begin. This very logical and simple system started with the early Mormon pioneers, as directed by Brigham Young. Nobody is about to change it. Ever.

Manti's main street, also U.S. 89, runs north and south. It's so wide, every block has a sign in the middle prohibiting U-turns. Easily, six motorhomes could be lined up abreast, with room to open doors, drop window awnings, and deploy a few pull-out barbecues.

Driving into town, fall colors were still in the trees, but most of it was on the ground. Carved pumpkins decorated the windows of tidy homes and businesses. A stubby limestone building topped with a steeple displayed two signs. One told of the present: American Legion Post 31. The other, a historic marker, told of a Presbyterian Church that had given up here thirty years ago.

The home of the Central Utah Ballet School also has a historic marker. Built in 1873, the building was once the oldest city hall in the state. When the city fathers moved out, they effectively tossed this old building in the trash, along with its heritage. It's in sad disrepair. But the ballet school goes on anyway. What are a few broken windows to kids, ages seven to nineteen, who spend their evenings and week-ends sharpening an athletic skill? Kids make choices with their free time based on what's around. Few towns offer a fine ballet school. But they all offer that of which tragic headlines are written. Someday, soon I hope, Manti's city fathers will wake up to the positive choices some of their kids have made and make a few of their own. This school de-serves better. In the meantime, everyone will enjoy the Nut-cracker Suite performed by these kids during the week of Christmas.

At the end of Main Street is the temple. It's awesome. It certainly has the ornate beauty of any classic cathedral or synagogue, but it does not have the same function. It is not a gathering place for communal worship. In fact, it is not even open on Sundays. A place of prayer, yes, but it is essentially a place for important religious ceremonies, like weddings and baptisms. It has no stained-glass windows, no bell tower, no pipe organ, no altar.

With its buttressed stone walls, three feet thick at ground level, it took an uncounted number of volunteers eleven years to build. Donated food and clothing were their only material compensation. Site preparation alone took two years, using horse-drawn scrapers and dynamite.

The temple shows no sign of age or weather. The lawn, which could sod a couple of football fields, has no brown spots. Obviously, its keepers care for it a great deal.

I knew the temple was closed to me and even to some Mormons. But the glass, revolving door showed a tastefully decorated foyer that had an inviting look about it.

The sun had just set and the lights were on inside. Other people were going in, so I did too. I was greeted warmly by Mr. Greenhalgh, a soft-spoken, retired schoolteacher, im-maculately dressed in a white suit, shirt and tie.

We sat in a quiet corner. (I am sure the temple has no other kind.) Mr. Greenhalgh told me that 560 volunteers run the temple. It's open five days and evenings a week. After it closes, an eight-person crew works all night scrubbing, vacu-uming, and polishing.

So much for what happened yesterday. Now that I have thawed out my water hose in Yogi Bear's shower again, the news is looking good. The snow has gone elsewhere. The sun is shining this morning.

"It's easy to find. Follow the feathers along the side of the road. They blow off the turkey trucks. And if the wind is right, just follow your nose." The cook at the senior center was giving me directions to a turkey farm.

She was right. White feathers line the roads wherever the flatbed turkey trucks have been. The trucks all go to Moroni, twenty miles north of here, where the birds are made oven-ready. This county produced 4.4 million turkeys last year, or 72 million pounds.

Pulling into the Shand farm in a little truck on loan from Yogi Bear, a tail-wagging sheepdog greeted me along with a million frantically gobbling turkeys. I learned later there were only 14,000 birds. They came hopping, running, half flying to crowd the fence. None of them faced me head on. With their heads cocked, they all stared at me, each using just one eye. More than have ever stared at me before.

A hawk flew over. Silence, for a few seconds. Then the gobbling began anew, but with a higher level of twitter.

Eighteen-year-old Travis Shand stuck his pitchfork in the ground. He appeared happy to stop what he was doing and talk with a stranger. He and Jeremy Keller, age nineteen, look after turkeys on two adjacent farms that belong to Travis's dad and his uncle.

Every year, well over 100,000 turkeys grow up here. The birds arrive as day-old chicks, the first brood in February. (The farm is closed in December and January.) How a chick producer can get 20,000 or so eggs to all hatch on the same day is beyond my comprehension. But they do. It takes seventeen to twenty-six weeks, depending on how big they want them, before the birds are trucked off to Moroni.

"If a little thing goes wrong, you can be sure they'll make the worst of it. Turkeys are dumb," Travis remarked. "I picked up a hen today that sat in a puddle and drowned. Maybe she fell asleep, I don't know. Anyway, she's history. They have heart attacks and just plain die if life gets to be too much for them, like if a jet flies over or a siren goes by."

The turkeys, the temple, and the nice folks of Manti were now behind me, where the winter winds blow. Rusty and I were on U.S. 89 again, headed south toward Interstate 15.

Now there I was, dead in the road, stopped behind a froth of bleating sheep. There must have been 200 of them. Three men on horseback and two happy dogs skillfully kept them tightly packed on the road and off the shoulders. The sheep, their woolly coats puffed up for the coming Utah winter, appeared to follow directions well. Ahead, they streamed into an open field.

Rusty perked her ears. She stood on the dashboard, taking it all in. Her tail wagged her body. She let out an occasional bark. I had to agree with her, it was a remarkable sight.

I guess sheepherders are a considerate bunch. Evidently, they did not want to delay a waiting cement truck and me. They pushed the sheep to move faster than the sheep wanted to go.

"Take your time," I said. Only Rusty heard me. "No hurry. Fact is, the cement probably has more important things to do today than we do."

61

Columbus Day is Transferable

Beaver, Utah

All city and county employees here work on Columbus Day, a national holiday. But come to Beaver two weeks from now, the first Monday of the deer hunt, and you won't find a government office open, except the post office. Even the schools will be closed.

Here in central Utah, as in small towns everywhere, people make trade-offs in their lifestyles—and their holidays—to get more of what they want. In fact, just living in a small town is a huge trade-off. Big-city amenities are given up: shopping malls, mail delivery, movie theaters, clinics, even the twenty-four-hour supermarket, access to which now seems an urbanite's birthright. In return, they get life at a slower pace, one filled with what is, to them, truly important. This may be as simple as knowing every kid on the high-school football team, not needing a key because you never lock your doors, making jam with homegrown strawberries, or just knowing the first name of every person you meet today. You better know, because they always know yours.

Much of what is important, of gut significance to the people here, lies in the Tushar Mountains just east of town. Peaks over 12,000 feet and places like Mount Holly, Puffer

Lake, Big John's Flat, Elk Meadows, and Merchant Valley give a map-reader's view of what's up there. A slick brochure tells of a "Mecca for recreation," the "state's largest mule-deer and elk herds," and "unsurpassed trout fishing." But all that's just a hint.

The wild sounds and scents of the high country and the memories of the excited laughter of his kids are what the mountains mean to John Christiansen. He has never seen them. He is blind. But he knows what's up there, how beautiful it is. On many visits over many years, his family has told him what they see.

The popular county attorney here for thirty-six years, John now has a private practice at age sixty-nine. He was pecking at his typewriter when I walked into his one-man office. John asked me to sit while he finished typing.

Those brief moments, watching him type, brought a jarring revelation. For a person who does not see what he types, to interrupt John in the process could disrupt his continuity. You and I can stop at any point and pick up where we left off simply by reading our last thought. John has to remember not only his last thought but also the last words he typed.

I looked around his basement office. Two small windows were near the ceiling. They did little more than indicate whether it was day or night outside. For John, I suppose, they did nothing at all. A big fluorescent fixture lit his office.

John lives five blocks from his office and walks it alone twice a day. He does not use a cane, doesn't even own one.

"There are no sidewalks here for a ways, so I walk on the side of the street," John explained. "What's under my feet tells me where I am. The road has a smooth, oiled surface, and it slopes to gravel. I can anticipate intersections pretty well."

"Ever get disoriented?"

"Oh, yes, but not often. I just stop and listen. The traffic tells me where I am," he said with a grin, "if there is any."

John answered the phone, apparently a client. Again, what you and I might write down as notes he has to commit to memory, even a phone number. He says that his typing was not as error-free as it once was. His part-time secretary checks it.

"The lights?" I ask without thinking.

Instantly I regretted it, knowing that I was prying and dwelling on his handicap. But John rescued me.

"You ask why I turn them on?" His warm smile got me through it. "If I don't, people think I'm not here. And, I confess, I do that once in a while." I think John enjoyed sharing a secret. It was a rich moment for me.

The merchants on Main Street look to the mountains for much of their business.

"Increasing mobility the last fifteen years has changed people's buying habits. The big out-of-town discounters have made it worse," the owner of a clothing store told me. "Now the tourist dollars determine for most of us if we have a good year, a bad year, or even if we will be in business for another one."

Clarence Pollard works his Main Street business in bib overalls. Below the bib, the overalls flow around a bulge that has developed over fifty-two years. He and his wife Kristine run Beaver Sport and Pawn. Among things lettered on the store's white front: Free Advice on Any Subject. Clarence and Kristine sell guns, fishing gear, and out-of-pawn items and run a small-loan business, accepting as collateral anything from real estate to a CD collection.

Complaining that nobody pawns things any more, Clarence pulled a power saw off a shelf. "This saw has been in this store six times. Each time I give him more money for it, because I want it. But it never fails, he always picks it up."

A lady next door, a joint auto-parts and Radio Shack store, came in to weigh a box on Clarence's bathroom scale, which he uses to weigh fish. "Did you hear Hugh got his elk with a bow and arrow?" she asked.

This is October. Hunting season.

In Beaver and the Tushar Mountains, nothing all year compares to it. First, it's elk season, followed by deer season, including a time for both archers and muzzleloaders. But the big hunt, the really big one, is the rifle deer hunt. It lasts only seven days.

"When it starts, this town will float in people with orange suits and California license plates," Clarence said. "It's probably the most festive time of the year. People prepare for this for months. Anticipation gets so hot, it will melt snow."

"It's not just a male thing, either," Kristine added. "Although it's a great sport that a father and son can do together, the whole family gets involved. It's the only time all year that the kids clean out the garage. They know if the truck backs in, it's loaded, and there better be room for a big buck."

The hunt begins at dawn on Saturday. The ladies tell me they will take over for the next couple of days. They will run the businesses. They will run the town. They will also shop.

"We figure if our husbands can spend $500 to go hunting, we probably can find something equally worthwhile for $500," Kristine joked.

We spent the next couple of nights in Beaver at a campground run by four ladies who came here from Phoenix. They all had jobs there in the Sunbelt and decided over a bowling game one night to start their lives over. They became partners. After some searching, they bought the Camperland RV Park here. That was over twenty years ago.

After the Columbus Day holiday that never was, this day started much the same but colder. Rusty and I walked from the campground as far as the H&H Rock Shop, named for Hattie and Hartley Greenwood. Their front yard is one rock pile after another, maybe a hundred, all separated by type. One was a pile of snowflake obsidian. Hattie said it is found only in Utah.

"We've been at it eighteen years," said Hattie. "The uglier the rock on the outside, the prettier it is on the inside. Did you know that?" Hattie showed me bookends made from various cut and polished rocks. She handed me one. "This is called petrified iron. You try and cut it, you will know where it got its name."

Two young kids were buying some sulfur from Hartley. They told us that they wanted to see if it really burns.

I asked Hattie if it did.

"Never tried to burn it. What I know about rocks is that they don't eat and they don't spoil. Nobody steals them, either."

She told me about another rock house here, reportedly the birthplace of Robert LeRoy Parker, better known as Butch Cassidy.

Barbara Bradshaw's grandfather was Butch Cassidy's cousin. She knows all about Butch Cassidy. While Rusty waited outside, Barbara and I sat in her living room and talked about Butch.

"When Butch would get in trouble," she recalled, "he would come over the hills. Grandpa would hide him in a shack down in the creek bed. Or he would cover him with hay, if the posse was close. Grandpa always said that Butch was a fine boy and a happy-go-lucky lad who never killed anyone. He got the name 'Cassidy' from a man he took up with who taught him to steal cattle. Then he started running with those four guys. They robbed trains and banks from Canada to Mexico. The Wild Bunch, they called them. One was the Sundance Kid. Sundance died up here around Pleasant Grove. Butch died around here, too, but nobody knows where."

"But the movie had them killed in Bolivia."

"Oh, forget that! They had to have a Hollywood ending, you know. He died at a different place and a different time. Butch visited up here when he was sixty-four years old. He always had a place to stay and a grubstake. Everybody loved Butch. I'm proud of him."

62

Truck Attack on the Library

Monticello, Utah

Before leaving Utah and going back home for winter clothes, I first wanted to visit Monument Valley. I stopped just north of there, on Highway 191, in a quiet little town named for the Virginia home of Thomas Jefferson. I never found out why, but I hung around long enough to turn up some other interesting things. It was not all that easy.

Monticello is the seat of San Juan County, the largest county in the state, 7,884 square miles. Still the courthouse, the sheriff's office, and two floors of county offices rarely make enough news in a week to fill half a page in the San Juan Record, which comes out every Wednesday.

This town of 2,000 has a conforming, laid-back way about it. And keeping it that way is probably the only thing that would get it exercised.

Here in Utah, seven out of every ten people are Mormons. In Monticello, it's closer to nine of every ten. If there is one tenet of the Mormon Church that is apparent to this outsider, it is the preeminence of the family. This may be why Utah has a literacy rate among the highest in the United States: 94 percent. The importance of good schools and libraries is obvious. It's especially true here in Monticello.

Their library is more than a book repository. Much of the town's heritage is there. In its foyer is a handmade replica of the town in miniature as it was about a hundred years ago. It covers a Ping-Pong-size table and is encased like a museum piece. Its layout was taken from old pictures, but its realism comes from the memories of those who made it.

TV tabloids will never find a lurid human drama here. Most people have never heard of Geraldo Rivera, or can't pronounce his name and don't care to be corrected. They live by the rules. Theirs are traditional, ordinary lives. Only ordinary things happen here.

That was until an eighteen-wheeler came into town with a driver who did not do the ordinary, even the logical, thing. He didn't set his brakes. He was parked next to the Texaco station on Main Street, better known as the Black Oil Parking Lot. It's a dirt lot that gradually slopes toward the street. Truck drivers park in the back of it all the time and go in the gas station for coffee or whatever.

Across the street from the lot is the San Juan County Library. It was a straight line the truck took, coasting across Main Street, over the curb, crashing into a huge tree. Had the tree not been there, the rig would have gone right through the front door, into the foyer of the library.

Rusty and I walked past the library last night. She was checking things with her nose. Even by streetlight, I could see where another truck had done the same thing. Except it hit a different tree and took off a major branch.

Dorothy Adams was the chair of the group who built the library in 1962. She is eighty-seven now.

From her front door, Dorothy led me to the kitchen of her comfortably furnished home. It has belonged to the Adams family for almost a century. Beautiful Navajo rugs cover her hardwood floors. They have been here sixty years. She has never taken them up. Dorothy never shakes them, claiming it breaks the weave. Cleaning is done with an electric broom, never a vacuum cleaner. Occasionally they get a shampoo, which Dorothy does on her hands and knees.

In the kitchen, Dorothy and a helper were busy cleaning up, putting dishes away and food in the refrigerator. I asked about the wild-truck attacks while nibbling on leftovers from a lady's luncheon that had just finished. Dorothy had ordered it from next door, an obvious advantage of living on the same block as Wagon Wheel Pizza.

"They leave the engines running in those big trucks, even when they are not in them," Dorothy said. "Don't you suppose things vibrate? Something gets them started so they roll freely like that."

"Possible. Once I can understand. But twice?"

She turned. A few red grapes went rolling across the floor. "Who told you twice? It has happened seven times."

"Seven times?"

That seemed impossible, at least beyond mere chance. Dorothy talked about it so casually, as if it were an everyday event. As yet, I'm not sure it wasn't.

"The last time, it was a brand-new truck on his first trip," a Peterbilt, coming from Idaho. "It crashed right into the reading room with a full load of potatoes. Books went all over the floor. Scared folks in there half to death. Can you imagine? That was in August, and the library is still closed."

"Covered by insurance?"

"Yes, but things are more important than money. We have no library now. And what if it had crashed into the foyer, if the little town had been destroyed? Well, that skill is gone. No one is left who could reproduce it."

While I was on my knees collecting grapes, Dorothy changed the subject. She told me that she has lived in this house since 1936, when she got married. It was the home of her husband's family. He was an attorney. As for her, "I'm a builder. It's an obsession. I have to build something all the time."

She led me out the side door to show me an obsessive project that was "just weeds and anthills when we started in 1988." It's now Pioneer Park: a stone fountain, gazebo, three small log buildings, and a little church. The church came first, built totally with volunteer labor and trees from the nearby mountains. Even the local teenagers got involved. They peeled the logs. Many of the logs in the other buildings, originally cabins built in 1918, Dorothy rounded up some place. Pee Wee Barela, who calls himself a general contractor but really is an artist, replicated a pioneer cabin, a tack shed, what he calls a "Spanish-American sod house." Its sod roof is so low, the house is hardly high enough to stand in.

Pee Wee said that the pioneers and cowboys who built and used these types of buildings didn't have carpenter's tools like levels or squares. So he didn't use them, either. He eyeballed it. Yet the sod house is only an inch and a quarter off square.

He got the name "Pee Wee" when he came here from New Mexico thirty years ago. "For some reason, they couldn't pronounce 'Isauro'."

The park, Dorothy said, belongs to the people of the town, but the land is still privately owned. "On Christmas Eve we have a live nativity scene in the park. It is really a beautiful event, but it's religious, you know. If this were public land, somebody would sue."

That comment surprised me. Not that church-and-state issues don't prompt lawsuits all over the country, but here in Monticello? I mean, this is God-fearing Utah, where the line between church and state is pretty thin.

What would Thomas Jefferson think?

Interestingly, the man who wrote the Declaration of Independence and lived in another Monticello was an outspoken advocate for the separation of church and state.

But Jefferson also wrote: "I tremble for my country when I reflect that God is just, that his justice cannot sleep forever."

What if Thomas Jefferson, the lawyer, were to try such a case in the county courthouse here? Joe-anti-nativity scene verses the Town of Monticello. Which side would he be on?

Wow! That would certainly shake things up and untie this unflappable town. They would get to know Geraldo Rivera personally, and Larry King, too.

Part VI

Arizona — Colorado — New Mexico

63

A Bad Day for Arizona

Flagstaff, Arizona

An airport near Interstate 40 reported wind gusts of forty-two knots, according to the National Weather Service. But for those of us who were out here in it, only the precise number was news. It blew out of the west, which was fine, even wonderful, since I was too. Nothing like a powerful wind behind a squared-ended motorhome. Life on the interstate doesn't get much better.

It was too good to last. At Flagstaff, I would leave Interstate 40 and head north up Highway 89. This course would put the wind exactly where I didn't want it. But life is still good. Before I got to the open expanse of the Coconino Plateau, where the wind blew free, I would find shelter in the Wilderness Mountains. Covering them is the largest stand of ponderosa pine in the world. Nature creates no better windbreak.

The day began clear and sunny, but at Flagstaff it turned gray and miserable. A pall of snow covered the town. I turned up the heater. Outside, people either scurried from place to place or were clenched together like cold fists. Snow began collecting at the bottom of the windshield. For a state that makes its living by being warm, it appeared that Arizona was having a bad day. This was early October, when seventy degrees is the norm here in Flagstaff.

Flagstaff is not typical of Arizona, though. Phoenix is. That sprawling Sunbelt mecca is in the low desert, 140 miles south of here. Flagstaff is 7,000 feet high. It has an average high temperature in January, for example, of forty-one degrees and a low of fourteen. North of town is Humphreys Peak at 12,643 feet, the highest point in the state. Up there at the Fairfield Snowbowl, they have three chairlifts and enjoyed cross-country skiing six months of the year.

Flagstaff is a big town, really, with 46,000 people. From the long string of headlights coming at me, it appears most of them are on the road this morning. Pregame shoppers, maybe? It's a football Saturday. They do have the homegrown Lumberjacks to root for. I just passed their campus at Northern Arizona University.

Leaving town, snow was still falling, but the flakes were dropping one at a time.

From her stretched-out travel position, Rusty was staring at me. Why do dogs do that? Staring back never affects her either way. She keeps doing it. It is interesting how long a stare can last without a blink. I am sure that dogs build up a memory bank of behavioral patterns of their masters. Drawing on that, they anticipate events or activities that affect them. For example, Rusty knows that when I open a closet door where her leash hangs she will probably be going for a walk. So she goes into her dance of anticipation. This staring may well be the loading process, the input into her data bank. But she is wasting her energy studying how I steer a motorhome. Then again, who am I to say?

If the stare means I want to stop and get out, then I got the message this time.

I took the route to Sunset Crater Volcano National Monument. The choppy road to the visitor center is a two-mile dish rattler. I stopped there to see what this place was about. Opening the door of the motorhome, a cold blast made a good case for putting on a jacket and persuaded Rusty to stay where she was.

"Its last eruption was 800 years ago," the man at the desk said. "But the lava flows near the cone look like they hardened just yesterday."

Apparently, tourists all ask the same questions, so he anticipated the next one.

"No, you can't look down in the volcano. You just look up at the rim, the volcanic cone."

Back in the motorhome, we bumped along another half mile, past the Bonito Lava Flow, an inhospitable volcanic landscape. At the look-up point, a one-mile foot trail loops around the base of the volcano. We got out. I considered taking Rusty on the self-guided nature walk, but a sign with a dog and a red line through it said that was a bad idea. It was nippy, anyway.

Sunset Crater formed when molten rock sprayed high into the air out of a crack in the ground. The molten rock quickly solidified, then fell to earth as cinders. As periodic eruptions continued over the next 200 years, heavier debris accumulated around the vent and created the 1,000-foot cone. In its most recent burst of activity, around the year 1250, lava containing iron and sulfur shot from the vent. According to the Park Service brochure, "the red and yellow oxidized particles fell back onto the rim as a permanent 'sunset,' so bright that the cone appears still to glow with intense volcanic heat."

Maybe it was too cold. The cone didn't glow. It just wasn't a good day in Arizona.

64

Indian Country

Tuba City, Arizona

On the Coconino Plateau, high winds persisted but the sky was clear. I set the speed control at forty-five mph. To go faster would tempt fate. Gusts moved the motorhome as if they had hooks. They were more comfortably managed at an easy pace.

With no traffic, there is nothing wrong with going slow. I turned off the radio and shut out all but the here and now, remembering what Emmy had said: "the traveler who misses the journey misses about all he is going to get."

Ahead, red-rock mesas interrupted the emptiness. But for the highway, the land was featureless.

It is a sad comment that so many people in modern America can't imagine a place like this, where you can gaze into infinity without fences, power poles, or houses to mar the view. Sadder still, few have any idea why it even matters.

Just before Cameron, I entered the great Navajo Nation. It is the largest of all Indian reservations, almost as big as West Virginia. It fills most of the northeastern part of Arizona. Covering 25,000 square miles, it spreads into neighboring New Mexico and Utah. At the center of the reservation is Hopi territory. It's a rectangle, the boundaries of which the tribes cannot agree upon. Although the Hopi have lived here longer than any other surviving people, they are now, by our decree, totally surrounded by their old enemies, the Navajo.

I passed through the Painted Desert. Wind had textured big drifts of orange sand into rills. Spaced sporadically along the edge of the highway were display stands made of scrap boards and flapping sheets of black plastic. Wind-blasted signs pitched so wildly that it was impossible to read what was for sale, or would be, on a better day.

In an earlier era, whites came through here in wagons to trade beads with Indian tribes that they knew little about. Now whites come to buy beads, driving sport utility vehicles named after Indians.

I arrived at Tuba City about sundown in a flurry of blowing sand. Founded in 1870 by Mormon missionaries and named for a Hopi chief, Tuba City is totally Navajo now.

The trading post here has been a landmark in Arizona since the 1880s. Now fully restored, it is perhaps the last remnant of Tuba City's Anglo heritage. Appropriately, McDonald's is across the street.

For one who lays low on holiday weekends, leaving them for crowds who use them as mini-vacations, my visit here was bad timing. Three tribal squad cars at the prime intersection in town were an indication. But I wrote it off as Saturday-night normal, until I learned that this was the final night of the week-long, Twenty-Ninth Annual Toh'nanees Dizi' Western Navajo Fair. The rodeo was already underway, as was the powwow at the high-school gym. The "redneck" country dance was next.

I hightailed it to the RV park behind the Quality Inn. There, the people in line at the check-in desk all spoke German. The two young girls running the place spoke English, the high-school variety.

A stupid policy of the Quality Inn threatened to turn a simple communication problem into an international incident, the Navajo Nation versus Germany. A key is required to turn on the water at each RV site, itself an inconsiderate and dim-witted idea. Obviously, if you are paying $19.50 for a full hookup, you want water. The Quality Inn wanted a deposit of $5.00 on the key. The Germans, three families in three motorhomes, apparently did not understand that the money would be refunded. Finally, it was agreed that they would rent one key for all three families to use.

My turn. I think the girls were relieved to see an American, native or otherwise.

Then one dropped a comment. "But you know, we are an hour behind Tuba City."

"Who is?" I asked, dumbfounded.

"The hotel, the trading post, the restaurant."

"Why is that?

"Tuba City is on daylight time."

"Aren't we in Tuba City?"

"Yes, but this is county land."

"It's not the reservation?"

"Yes, but the county is on mountain time."

"Oh, so the whole reservation in on daylight time."

"Yes, except for right here."

"Isn't that confusing?"

"No, we're used to it."

"I mean for customers."

"Don't know. Why should it be?"

That's the way that day ended. I climbed into bed, telling Rusty I wouldn't want to live it over.

65

Mostly Texans Here

Dolores, Colorado

The next day, a much better one, I crossed the Navajo
Nation. On the other side, Highway 160 cuts across the
corner of New Mexico before entering Colorado. I was
headed for a Colorado town named Dolores. By day's end, I
set up housekeeping there next to the Delores River at the
Outpost Motel and RV Park.

An interesting thing about this town: after forty-eight
hours here, I had met more Texans than locals, of which
there are 986. I can say the same for guys from Arkansas and
Louisiana. Orange hats and camouflage pants are everywhere.
It's deer-hunting season.

They pull in here at the RV park red-eyed and unshaven
in anything that has four-wheel drive and a trailer hitch.
Behind them, under waterproof tarps on flat hay trailers, are
what they have packed for a week in the mountains and
maybe a couple of all-terrain vehicles. Five-gallon cans lined
the back of one trailer—two for gas, twelve for water. Long
horse trailers, their roofs covered with bales of hay, haul
horses and mules. Several pickups carried electric generators.
Not just for campsite power, they are to operate refrigerated
compartments on the way home, a nonstop trip that can take

eighteen to twenty-four hours. The sport may be in the hunt, but on home turf, the fresh venison and elk in those coolers are what they have to show for their week in the Colorado Rockies.

Main-street Dolores loves them.

At Wagons West you can buy a sweatshirt fronted with an elk for $34.99, or for $75.00, a two-holed birdcage. Incidentally, the birdcage is made of rare, old barn boards and is dated and signed. Proprietor Sondra Childs calls the deer hunt "our Christmas."

On a table out front, at the edge of the parking lot, is an electric roasting oven like the one my mother used for cooking the Christmas turkey. Sondra has it bubbling with ham and beans. It draws the orange-hat crowd like free drinks in a Vegas casino. And Sondra knows her customer's tastes. Next to the pepper is a bottle of McIlhenny's Tabasco Sauce.

Before noon today, Sondra took in $8,000 just on hunting licenses. A $95,000 day is not hard to do during hunting season. Contrast that with one day last winter when she took in just 34 cents. Her friend had bought a candy stick. Her store will stay open until midnight tonight. "Hunters just drive until they get here, which can be anytime. So we adjust," Sondra explained.

As do the gals at the Ponderosa Restaurant. "They ask us what time we open. We ask them what time they want breakfast. They say 5:00, so we open at 4:30." The waitress who told me that was still bright-eyed. The season, however, was just beginning. They close at 10:00 p.m. and keep those long hours throughout the month-long hunt.

At the Outpost, Ray and Darlene LeBlanc's ten motel units and three cabins are booked a year in advance. While sheets tumbled in the dryer, Darlene rested for a few minutes. "It's an exciting time with all the goings on. Many of the fellows don't even stay here. They just stop for showers. We keep a room open for them. They wash up, make phone calls, and they're gone 'til next year."

"No women?" I asked.

"Ninety-five percent are men, maybe more. But have you noticed each group is a family? Father, sons, cousins, sometimes grandsons. It's really neat."

A hunter from Austin, Texas, told me that he has horses trained for roping but wouldn't bring them up in these mountains. "They might get hurt, for one thing. A mountain horse, now, you can't believe what it can do. They'll take ya straight up, even better than those things." He pointed to a Polaris 4X4 in the back of a pickup. It appeared as two seats atop four balloon tires.

"That gang from East Texas brought horses."

"Maybe those boys have worked them in the mountains somewhere, though there's nothing like these where they live. A horse is good, don't get me wrong. They walk up on a deer and won't spook it. I mean close enough to kill it. But unless a horse is gun-broke, you better get off to shoot. You can train a horse to do anything but stand still."

For the rest of the day, they came off the mountain. Mud hung everywhere, even on side mirrors. Rusty teamed up with two other dogs to form a greeting party. Darlene's dalmatian, on just three legs (she was hit by a car), set the pace. It was like a homecoming.

The river flowing through town took its name from two Catholic priests who passed through here in 1876. They gave it a long Spanish name that ended with the word Dolores. Translated, the name meant "The River of the Lady of Sorrow." Colorful as it may have been, that long name did not survive the last century. So, in the finest tradition of American place-names, Colorado now has a river, a town, and even a county named Dolores.

Because Dolores lies in a narrow river valley, it comes and goes in only two directions, stretching along Railroad and Central Avenues. The next morning, I walked into town along Railroad, also Highway 145. Before 1953, a walk here would have been along the tracks of the Rio Grande Southern Railroad (RGSRR).

"I remember my dad saying, 'If I knew I was going to take it up, I wouldn't have put it down so well.' His last days

on the job were spent pulling up the track that he had
worked to keep down his whole life. He came here in 1916,"
Ruby Gonzales told me.

Ruby, at age sixty-four, is a volunteer at the Dolores
Visitor's Center, where we met. It's in a Victorian-style building, a replica of the town's original train depot. Inside are
pictures of Dolores' railroading days, which began in 1891.

"My maiden name is Vigil," Ruby had said. I thought that
an unusual caveat but said nothing about it until I began
looking around the depot and reading captions under the
pictures. There were pictures of Alex Vigil, the yard foreman,
and of him and his crew struggling in the snow to put
derailed equipment back on the track.

Along one wall is a diorama, a three-dimensional miniature scene of the town as it was in 1946. Ruby pointed out
the section-house where she was born, a wood-frame home
with three bedrooms, one bath, and a wood-stove. She said
her dad brought home old creosote-treated ties for firewood.
"Boy, did they ever burn!" Ruby remembered.

I examined the line of little white section-houses. "You
say there were ten kids in your family?"

"We weren't all there at once."

"It wasn't crowded?"

"Probably! We were also poor, but I didn't know it then."

Ruby's dad and his crew, kept the railroad safe and operating for over half a century. The train ran once a day, up
2,233 feet of mountain and down again, connecting the remote towns of Durango, Mancos, Dolores, Rico, Telluride,
and Ridgeway. None of them were or are significant cities of
the West. But they are still there.

On a narrow-gauge piece of track, in front of the visitor's
center, rests Galloping Goose Number Five. It is being restored, which it sorely needs. Built on the body of a 1926
Pierce-Arrow limousine, it earned its name by galloping along
the rails at the ungainly gait of a goose, so they say. From
1931 to about 1950, seven such one-car "motor-trains" carried
passengers, mail, and light freight up and down the RGSRR
system. One ran every day. It was a rough ride. I was told of

a man who rode it from here to Stoner, a thirteen-mile trip. He refused to ride it back, so he walked.

As states go, Colorado and Texas are decisively different. Roads go up and down in one, into the sunset in the other. Texas is so big it takes dawn nearly an hour to cross it. Colorado is so high, parts of it have winter weather all year.

In the fall, right here by the Dolores River, they meet and connect. People from these two unrelated states share common ground. Ground literally, but more like space, as in vast, unrelenting, awesome, and wild. Whether it nurtures pine trees or cactus, space is the essence of the American West. It reduces a man to a common level and pushes him to a greater reliance on himself.

These are an unfettered sort here. They know their limits and those of the wilds. Otherwise they would not have come to these rugged mountains either as hunters or homesteaders.

66

The Anasazi: Now We Know

Mesa Verde National Park

Another thing about the American West: if John Wayne or Jimmy Stewart didn't tell us about it, then it never happened. As for the really olden days, like in the time of Moses or a few centuries afterward, everything supposedly happened on far-off continents. It fell to Charlton Heston and Cecil B. DeMille to fill us in on those. That's just the way it was.

None of those emissaries of the Old West, nor their contemporaries like Randolph Scott and Henry Fonda, had ever heard of Mesa Verde. Nor Charlton Heston, for that matter. At least if they had, they never let on. As a result, millions of us grew up lacking a true perspective, the big picture of the Old West.

In fairness to history teachers, they certainly told us. National Geographic and Life, which everybody saw when I was a kid, had pictures of the cliff houses here in Colorado. In fact, some of these prehistoric dwellings were still being discovered in the forties and fifties and were making news then.

Getting it from a flat page, however, was not the same. To have meaning and relevance, history had to be multidimensional, with music and fistfights. It had staying power only if we learned it in the dark, from those extraordinary ladies and men who really lived it.

What happened here around 750 a.d., I think, got jumbled in the classroom with algebra formulas. It remained as knowledge probably just long enough for the final exam, at least in my case.

What's more, we could see it for ourselves: there was nothing out here but wide-open spaces. It was just cowboys and Indians, horses and buffalo. Nobody else was here or ever had been. That's just the way it was.

My history refresher began in the visitor center in Mancos, a town of 950 people in the southwest corner of Colorado. It started with coffee and zucchini bread served by the volunteer hostess, a retired stewardess from the DC-6 days, when first class was the whole plane. She also gave me a big napkin decorated with the brands of the cattle ranches in "Four Corner Country." (The Four Corners are eighty miles southwest of here in the Navajo Nation. It's the only spot in our country where four states meet: Colorado, New Mexico, Arizona, and Utah.)

Handing me brochures, she tossed off a comment. "More people lived here 1,500 years ago than now, more than twice as many, even at the peak of our tourist season."

"Lived where?" I asked, not sure what she had said.

"Here in Montezuma County."

"Where in Montezuma County?"

"Mostly up there on the mesa," she pointed out the window, "now Mesa Verde National Park. It's in those brochures."

They were the ancestral Puebloans, or Anasazi, a Navajo word meaning "the ancient ones," sometimes interpreted as "the ancient enemies." They arrived here about 400 a.d., give or take a few centuries. They mysteriously went away, leaving as if on vacation, around 1500 a.d.. Having no known enemies, they farmed the mesa tops and hunted the canyons. Growing in numbers to maybe 5,000, they first lived in cleverly vented, covered holes in the ground that we latecomers call pit houses. Later they built stone dwellings using stone tools.

Most lived on the mesa, but a few lived in elaborate stone villages built into the sheltered recesses of canyon walls. These cliff dwellings became their legacy. Some of them are still 90 percent intact. Interestingly, these dwellings were discovered less than a hundred years ago by a couple of cowboys looking for stray cattle. Unlike many of our "discoveries" in the West, the Indians never told anyone about them. Some speculate that Mesa Verde was forbidden land in the Indian world, never to be discussed or visited, the remains of an ancient culture best left alone.

Despite decades of careful excavation and analysis, archaeologists say we will never know the whole story of the Anasazi. They left nothing scratched on rocks or in writing. Much that was important in their lives has perished.

Yet for all their silence, these ruins speak with a certain eloquence. They tell of people adept at building, artistic in their crafts, skillful in wresting a living from a difficult land. The Anasazi of Mesa Verde were apparently the heirs of a vigorous civilization that originated somewhere else. Their accomplishments in community living and the arts rank among the finest expressions of human culture in ancient America, if not the world.

Established as a national park in 1906, Mesa Verde was designated a World Heritage Culture Park in 1978 by UNESCO, an organization of the United Nations. So it is now a site of international significance. It ranks up there with the pyramids of Egypt, set aside to preserve the early works of humankind.

This day was quickly passing. I thanked the stewardess and headed for the mesa. It's only seven miles ahead. I looked for a RV park along the way. I found one that had shut down, another that might just as well be. The campground inside the park at Morefield Village, I discovered, was closed for the winter.

Towering over me was the mesa. The setting sun had turned it to rust. I imagined a city there, families living in a crevice or a hole in the ground, comfortable, warm, probably wanting for little. Their spirits, looking down, surely chuckled. Here was I: frustrated for lack of a ready spot to plug in my motorhome. I didn't need much. Just heat for the night, a market wrap-up on CNN, maybe a rerun of Seinfeld, a warm shower and coffee in the morning.

Near the park entrance on Highway 160, RVs situated up a rutted driveway looked friendly. It turned out to be the suburbia of Mesa Verde. Many of those who work at the park, for its private concessionaire, live right here. Since park jobs are seasonal, they spend the summer here, living conveniently in their RVs with hookups provided by their employer. Come the end of October, just a couple of days from now, they head elsewhere for the winter.

Gwen and Bob Bills were walking down the rutted road from their Bounder as I walked up. We met halfway. Within minutes, my luck turned for the better. Not only was I assured of hot coffee and a shower in the morning, but I was to see first-hand what John Wayne never showed me.

Retired from the corporate world, Gwen and Bob were tour guides. Tomorrow, Gwen was conducting an all-day tour, the last one of the year. I would join her. She loaded me with books and an overnight reading assignment. Then they pointed me to the A&A Mesa Verde RV Park next door, which I mistook earlier for just a mini-golf course and riding stable.

"Somehow I missed the sign," I told Ray Huseby when I checked in.

Ray and his brother brought their dad and their families here three years ago to get their kids out of Denver. "It got so my son was scared to go to school," Ray said. "They have really flowered here." And well they should, with horses and dirt bikes and everywhere a nonthreatening wilderness in which to ride them.

Ray built not just a forty-five-site campground but a family park. Every night in the summer he hooks his tractor to a wagon, loads it with kids, and goes on a fossil hunt, leaving the adults to unwind around the campfire.

I met Gwen at the appointed 8:30 A.M. She had the heater running in the big Bluebird bus. The 1,000-foot climb, winding to the mesa top, took thirty minutes and made a noisy case for rear-mounted engines. Yelling over the diesel roar, Gwen said the park had a fire in August 1996 that uncovered 411 new archaeological sites. The firefighters on the ground were not too thrilled with the help they got from the water-dropping helicopters. It seems that they got their "water" from a sewage pool.

Gwen picked up her tour group at the Far View Lodge, the only motel in the park. The rest of the day was divided between today and fifteen centuries ago.

Some cliff houses we studied from across a canyon, others we stood next to and looked inside.

At the Spruce Tree House—each cliff dwelling has a name—Gwen told us that the Anasazi tossed their trash close by. Scraps of food, broken pottery, tools, anything unwanted went down the slope in front of their houses. Much of what we know about their daily life comes from their garbage heaps. The Anasazi also kept turkeys and dogs as pets but Gwen didn't say how we know that.

I did get some firsthand information, though, from park ranger Michael Groomer at the Spruce Tree House.

"We have a phone for emergencies," he told me. "I got a call one day from a lady named Betty. She was with AT&T and wanted to talk with the resident at this number. I told her that they left 700 years ago. She just said, 'Well, I'll call later.' I told her that I really did not expect them later, or anytime in the future. You know how those telemarketing people are. They don't give up. So she asked me to take a message. I told her, 'Sure, but I don't have a stone to write with.' She went away."

He said that the phone is hidden, but the line is visible in places. When visitors ask about it, he tells them that the cliff people had cable TV. "You know what?" Michael laughed, "some people believe it!"

He went on: "They ask me why they built their cliff dwellings so far from the highway. And why the people back then only built ruins. One guy asked me to settle an argument. He wondered if I knew at what elevation deer become elk. I am still wondering where that idea comes from. Of course, when I tell people the number of known archaeological sites here on the mesa, someone invariably asks me the number of unknown sites. I just say that we are still looking for them."

Jimmy Stewart would have loved it.

67

Ten-Cent Coffee

Continental Divide, New Mexico

I heard reports of snowstorms around me, so I headed south, deep into New Mexico. I stopped in Gallup, on the western edge of the state. Rusty and I walked around town. I made some instant coffee and decided that is all I would do here.

I turned east on Interstate 40 toward Albuquerque. New Mexico was new to me. This is the seventh state I have visited since I started this rambling trek last April. Seven states in seven months. Sounds like a slogan for a commercial tour director. But no travel agency could package this tour. Who would buy it? No American tourist, certainly. He wants seven states in seven days. Or better yet, a lifetime of adventure in two weeks, the thrills of risking his life without taking any risk at all.

For me, it's been perfect. Creating memories are what these days are for. Tomorrow, this day will be forever one of them. I will make the most of it while it's still here.

Alongside the road, big, gaudy signs overwhelm nature. Their black-on-yellow letters told where to buy. Along the bottoms red strips told how many miles to get there. Carved onyx. Zuni silver. Cactus candy. Kachina dolls. Desert honey. The last one has a big arrow and the words Exit Here.

I followed the red arrow and parked by a historic marker in front of a curio shop, or trading post, as they like to call them. Spread before me was a painted fence of signs, behind which rose the tops of three fake teepees. Along with souvenirs, film, and a Navajo rug weaver, the fence advertised coffee at ten cents.

I got out to read the marker, carrying the remains of my coffee from Gallup. I was at an elevation of 7,275 feet, straddling the Continental Divide.

This was the same stony backbone of the North American continent that I stood upon at South Pass, Wyoming. But this spot has been gussied up. The marker reads: "Rainfall divides at this point. That falling on the west side flows into the Pacific Ocean; that falling on the east side flows into the Atlantic." I did the natural thing, what any curious tourist would do. I poured the rest of my coffee on the great divide. It hit the ground and disappeared.

Recognized now with its own zip code, the town here, called Continental Divide, goes back to the days of Route 66. Part of the original thoroughfare is still here, paralleled by its replacement, Interstate 40. These roadside curio shops, those that have survived, also date back to those days.

I am getting the message loud and clear that this journey is becoming a circle that is closing in. Geography is telling me something, or maybe preparing me for it. First the Continental Divide, now the Mother Road again.

"Even if you don't like coffee, you can't pass it up for a dime," said the lady behind the case of turquoise jewelry.

Why does she sound like a recording?

I drew some self-serve coffee that was inconveniently but strategically located in the back corner of the store. To get there, I passed by racks of merchandise. This was no subtle Indian trick. It came right from the pages of Marketing 101. "To get the milk and eggs, the customer must pass through the isles of junkfood."

I went back up front to punch the lady's reset button and get her out of automatic.

"Which direction does the water go when it rains?" I asked.

That did it, all right. Her whole expression changed.

"Been so long since it's rained," she said, apparently pausing apparently to think about the question. "You read the sign out there, I bet?" She pointed toward the marker.

"Yep, it says that you are perched right on the watershed."

"Guess so. And they say up here that water goes out of a toilet clockwise on one side of the divide and counterclockwise on the other side. But I've never really watched it." She chuckled at the prospect.

"I think someone is confusing the Continental Divide with the equator," I replied, letting that subject drop.

En route to more Native American coffee, I rubbed a coonskin cap from Turkey, shook a rubber snake from China, and fingered some arrowheads handmade in Mexico. On the jewelry counter was a dish of "rose pods" made back east somewhere. Each the size of an egg, a rose pod is compressed sawdust impregnated with a fragrance. Once it gets on your hands, I found, it's hard to get off.

Back in the motorhome, eastbound, I noticed that Route 66 continued to parallel the interstate. So I pulled off at Thoreau and transferred to the old migrant trail to see how far it would take me.

68

The Uranium Rush of 1950

Grants, New Mexico

Thirty miles later, Route 66 became Santa Fe Avenue, the main street of Grants, once the "Carrot Capital" and more recently the "Uranium Capital." I decided to explore this place to see why now it's just the county seat. Tomorrow, that is.

I hitch a ride into town early the next morning with the folks from Ciboloa Sands RV Park. Empty storefronts, alternating with vacant lots, spread along Santa Fe Avenue for a couple of miles. Obviously, this town of 9,000 once had many more.

It started as "Grant's Camp," named for the three Grant brothers who were building a railroad. It evolved to "Grant's Station," then to just "Grant's." The post office removed the apostrophe in 1937, protesting that towns don't have apostrophes.

Active tracks of the Santa Fe parallel Santa Fe Avenue, but trains don't stop here anymore. The train depot is just another anonymous main-street building. Across the street, however, the Grants Station Restaurant is probably busier today than the old depot ever was.

About ten years ago, Bud and Shirley Rieck decided the town should preserve its railroad heritage. Bud has always been in the food business, so they bought a vacant Denny's and scrounged railroad memorabilia to decorate it. Most of it was given to them, like the 1912 Santa Fe sign that someone literally ripped off the side of the train depot. When it arrived in bits and pieces, Bud spent a whole night gluing it together. It's now a prime showpiece in the Grants Station Restaurant.

At the table next to me sat a trucker, a school administrator, a miner, and a fourth man, identified only as a Democrat—all retired. They were engaged in a serious, about-to-be-table-pounding argument over the distance to the nearby Indian casino. I interrupted and asked them about the heyday of uranium. Apparently it was an easy transition. The casino forgotten, the subject changed instantly.

"After Paddy Martinez came into town with a chunk of uranium ore, the place went nuts. Prospectors fumbling with Geiger counters were stumbling over each other, trespassers were getting shot at, and the lawyers had a field day. That was in 1950," one man proclaimed.

Instantly, the others jumped on him. "No, no, it was earlier."

They went at it again. I learned that the uranium industry here created 7,000 jobs between 1955 and 1985. This area produced 65 percent of this country's uranium and grew from 1,500 to 15,000 people. After the meltdown scare at Three Mile Island in 1979, the price of uranium went down, layoffs here went up, and Grants soon shrunk by one-half.

Hiking back to the RV park, I fought a head wind that was no everyday mesa duster. The outer spin of a Pacific hurricane off Mexico, it had an unobstructed run at me across a 376,000-acre bed of lava. No frozen lake could have given the wind a more bitter bite. The Spanish called this hostile expanse El Malpais, which in their language means "the badlands." During that bone-chilling trek, I, too, found some names for it in my language.

The wind blew across El Malpais for three more days. The rain came, then the snow. Rusty and I played in it. It was like being a kid again back in Duluth, Minnesota. Of course, in

New Mexico I did not have to wait five months for the snow to melt.

On the third night of the storm, a sudden silence awakened me. The blower in my electric heater had stopped. At first I thought the park had lost power but soon discovered that the repeated rocking of the motorhome in the high wind had worked my power cord out of the receptacle. An easy fix, and back to bed. Life's problems are so simple out here.

During the storm, vehicles came and went. Those of us with no schedule chose to wait it out. We all got to know each other. The cable-TV system in the park included the Weather Channel. We in our warm nomadic homes watched as the storm swirled in bright colors, dumped on us, and moved east.

By late afternoon of the fourth day, the low clouds moved out, leaving behind mountains covered with gleaming snow. I had not seen them before. Sundown briefly spread them with color. Then they disappeared.

69

On the Santa Fe Trail

Las Vegas, New Mexico

R usty, the ever-silent observer, always knows early when it is time to break camp. Once the process starts, she is constantly in the way. I stumble over her occasionally. She must have a deep-seated fear that I will leave without her unless she keeps bumping into me, reminding me that she is here.

I said good-bye to my fellow hostages of the storm. We chugged out of Grants. Rusty finally settled in her seat. We headed east toward Albuquerque, directly into the fireball. Even with sunglasses, I had to block the glare with my hand. The sun was warm and reassuring. It was good to shake off cabin fever and get back on the road. I love this lifestyle.

Interstate 40 makes a straight shot across New Mexico, skirting its biggest city, and then on into Texas. It ends on the other side of the continent. No country on earth has a highway network as convenient and efficient as our interstate system. Then again, few need one. Without any real plan, I turned north on Interstate 25 where it crosses Interstate 40 at Albuquerque.

It was sixty miles to Santa Fe, a favorite locale for those who write the travel section for the Sunday paper. Multiculturalism, the enduring essence of New Mexico, is apparently the soul and charm of this city of 56,000 people. Now the state capital, parts of it have been around for four centuries. I have heard too much about Santa Fe to even be curious about it. I didn't stop. Perhaps I should have. I know my well-traveled friends will shake their heads when I tell them that I drove right by it.

Instead, we continued on another sixty-five miles to Las Vegas, which in the 1880s was one of the roughest towns on the frontier. About this town I was curious.

I pulled into a near-empty RV park, put Rusty on a long leash, and took off on foot to explore this hangout of "Doc" Holliday and Billy the Kid. I quickly discovered Las Vegas was better known as a mercantile center on the Santa Fe Trail.

The Victorian-style houses along Seventh Street have deep front yards, covered today with long shadows. Built around 1920, nothing man-made separates them, except some landscaping. There are no fences or walls.

Dry leaves under my feet make that pleasant crunching sound of late fall. Their warm colors spread over the gray sidewalk, humped in spots to almost stumbling height by the swelling roots of street-side elm trees.

If the behavior of its dogs tells anything about a neighborhood's peace with itself, Seventh Street is secure and content. Two dogs slept in front of one house. The eye of another, a golden retriever, tracked me as I stepped over him. His tail, thumping the sidewalk, scattered the dry leaves. A frisky sheepdog joined me when I turned onto National Street, but he tired of me after only a block.

I felt sorry that I left Rusty behind. She would have liked Seventh Street.

I walked across the campus of New Mexico Highlands University. National becomes Bridge Street, a logical name change as it crosses the Gallinas River, little more than a marsh-wetting brook. Residents call this Old Town. The sidewalk along here has stubby iron pegs sunk in its outer edge.

They anchor iron rings that were once used for tying horses, mules, and oxen.

For many years, Old Town was designated West Las Vegas. Long before that, it was called Nuestra Senora de las Dolores de Las Vegas (Our Lady of Sorrows of the Large Meadows). Until 1970, the only thing it shared with East Las Vegas was a name. Two very independent towns, run by two separate governments, divided by the thin Gallinas River, the old and the new, the traditional and the novel, the Hispanic and the Anglo.

Las Vegas goes back to when New Mexico was part of Old Mexico. In 1835, Mexican settlers came to these meadows as part of a land grant from their government. There were fewer than fifty of them, just fifteen families. In the Spanish manner, they laid out a large plaza, which today is the centerpiece of Old Town. Flat-roofed log and adobe houses, sharing common walls, formed a defensive enclosure. The fortlike structure had only two entrances. In case of an Indian attack, their livestock could be herded inside and the entrances blocked.

For many years, Las Vegas was the end of the Santa Fe Trail, which started in Independence, Missouri. The arrival in the plaza of caravans from the east was a festive occasion, with traders setting up their merchandise in the fashion of a farmers market. Townspeople put on lively fandangos to entertain travel-weary Americanos.

The Santa Fe Trail brought jobs to Las Vegas and guns to the Indians. But by then the U.S. Army was moving in. New Mexico became a U.S. territory in 1848. This little Hispanic town of 1,000 people was its major trade center.

"But then the railroad came," said Jack Lamstra, a history buff and a restorer of stone structures. He describes himself as a masonry-building junkie in paradise. "With the railroad came the cultural collision between the Americans and the Hispanic land-grant community, who had sunk deep roots here by then." In 1879, Las Vegas saw its first iron horse. The territory got its first railroad town. The newcomers the railroad brought were products of America's maturing industrial society. Their mentality was one of competition and profit. Their values clashed with the self-sufficient, agrarian culture of the town's founders.

When the railroad bypassed the Old Town Plaza and ended a mile east of the Gallinas River, a new boomtown was born. They called it the City of Las Vegas at first. What happened to that presumptuous title is unclear. Perhaps the town just did not live up to it. Anyway, it evolved into East Las Vegas.

Immediately the territory's first telephone system and opera house were established in the new Anglo community. It became a fashionable commercial and residential district by Eastern standards, in sharp contrast with West Las Vegas. By 1882, the combined towns grew to about 6,000 people, rivaling Denver, El Paso, and Tucson in size.

Strategically located on both the Santa Fe Trail and the Atchison, Topeka, and Santa Fe Railroad, Las Vegas was hit by everything untamed and lawless in the Old West. Some said that all the riffraff from Dodge City and other Kansas cow towns came here on the first train that summer of 1879.

"Doc" Holliday practiced a little dentistry and ran a saloon and gambling hall here. But he left town after shooting a drunken cavalry veteran in front of his place. Jesse James, who kept a low profile under an assumed name, vacationed with his gang at the hot springs north of town. Lawman Pat Garrett shot it out at the train depot with a lynch mob that wanted to remove prisoners from his custody. And Billy the Kid complained about his accommodations at the Las Vegas jail, saying, "It is a terrible place to put a fellow in."

Fed up with what was happening in their town, a motivated group of citizens began dragging prisoners out of jail and hanging them from the windmill that stood in the plaza. They usually just cleaned out the jail, hanging whoever was there. On one occasion, they strung up three at once. (Children reportedly hanged dogs from the windmill in copycat fashion.)

A second group of townspeople disapproved of the hangings and tore down the windmill to stop them. That didn't accomplish much. Group one then began lynching their victims from telegraph poles and bridges. The word eventually got around in outlaw circles that Billy the Kid was right about Las Vegas being a terrible place.

I wandered around the tree-lined plaza. Classic, century-old buildings surround it. The original adobe ones went long ago. The Plaza Hotel is now the biggest. Built in 1882, it is one of 908 buildings in this town on the National Register of Historic Places.

In the 1950s, a shortsighted trend to modernize decimated the old hotel. Its original tin ceilings were covered, its floor-to-ceiling windows were filled with brick and mortar, and its elegant twin staircases were closed off. Shag carpet covered the hardwood floors. The finest hotel in New Mexico territory was now just another beer bar with a hamburger grill.

Fortunately, that uninspired trend of covering the past with gloss paint and glass brick has been reversed, and none too soon. The fourteen-foot ceiling in the hotel lobby again displays a pattern created in tin by an artist of the last century. The wide wood staircases now lead to thirty-eight sunlit guest rooms. The shag carpet has gone to a landfill.

Just off the plaza, a one-time cowboy has a store of antiques and barn and attic clean-outs. Surprisingly, he is not too keen on selling any of them. I picked up an issue of Life dated August 12, 1946. It sported a black-and-white picture of Loretta Young on the cover. I asked him the price.

"Kind of hate to sell that. Once it's gone, I may never get another one."

"Then why not just call this place a museum and charge admission?" I whimsically replied.

"You a wise guy, or something?" he snapped.

I sensed we were not getting on too well, but I wanted to hear about his days as a cowboy. He said he hated all cows and most people but liked horses. He drew a picture of a horse's eye on the back of an unopened telephone bill to graphically display why a horse has such wide peripheral vision. Having an eye on each side of your head is a good enough explanation, I suppose, but he had his theory.

And another theory. "An old-time cowboy walks ramrod straight from being on a horse so much. These new cowboys ride a pickup all day and walk bent over."

I admitted that I had never noticed. I hoped he would stand up so that I could check his posture. But he spent the whole time in a chair by the door, within reach of his coffee, an ashtray, his mail, and a radio. I never saw a cash register.

70

A Route around Albuquerque

Vaughn, New Mexico

We got started late the next day, sometime after lunch. People in the workaday world had faced a decision or two by now. I had not, but was about to. How do I get from westbound Interstate 40 to southbound Interstate 25 without going through Albuquerque?

Competing in the motorhome with the thank-god-it's-Friday crowd through the city that has a third of the state's population was not my idea of how to spend happy hour. Besides that, the sun was in my eyes again. So I cut south on Highway 54 at Santa Rosa.

Like most old highways of the Southwest, it runs parallel to the railroad tracks, confirming one of my platitudes of the road: Once the way is made, we all follow. Rushing water was the continent's first trailblazer. Animals were next, then the Indians, the foreign explorers, the wagon masters, the railroad builders, the engineers of highway departments, and now the rest of us.

On this flat, shackless grassland, even the impersonal freight trains of the Santa Fe are welcome, hinting of life. All going the other way, they pass about as often as a car.

Ten minutes into this course change, I began to regret it. A heavy wind out of the west slowed me to forty miles per hour. Strong gusts whipped the wires of my mirror-mounted antennas against the motorhome, which increasingly showed a mind of its own about where we are headed.

Still fighting the sun, now at dashboard level, I stopped at Vaughn, a junction. Highways 54 and 60 meet here. I pulled onto a gravel area next to the town's only AAA-rated motel. It seemed a comfortable rest stop for conventional travelers, those who must unpack a suitcase before even brushing their teeth. I was beat, ready to start my Friday happy hour and let the wind and the rest of the day blow themselves out.

After clicking the volume down on The Ricki Lake Show, the lady at the motel desk said that she had not heard a weather forecast. "But I've lived here a long while and know about our winds. They stop at night, sometimes. Then sometimes they don't," she explained, offering me coffee left from the morning shift.

Recognizing my visit was not for motel business, she reached for the remote control and punched the volume up. "Will ya look at that?" Her hand swept toward the TV. "Where do you suppose they get these people who talk about their personal lives like that, in front of everybody? Those three women," she now shook a flyswatter at the TV, "all say they are jealous of gay men. Now, what in the world is that about?"

"You don't have that kind around here?"

"You kidding! Have them around here?" She glared at me. "I didn't know they existed until I got this job and started watching TV all day."

She suggested that I park for the night by the Shell Food Mart. It would be quieter there, she insisted.

While I was in the motel, an empty stake truck pulled in near my motorhome. It had Mexican license plates. Two men were under it.

"We make it work," a third man offered in very timid and labored English. I think he expected me to run him off. I wished them luck and left for the Shell Food Mart. So much for my first face-to-face encounter with NAFTA, our recent free-trade treaty with Mexico.

I woke only once during the night. A truckload of cattle had stopped upwind of me. You never know how many air holes there are in a buttoned-up motorhome until that happens. Whether it was the smell or the noise of the cows banging around on the steel deck, I got up to check on the weather. No change.

71

Where Dust Bunnies Can't Hide

Mountainair, New Mexico

Wide awake and ready at 5:00, I picked up Highway 60 again against a lesser wind. Because it was dark, it seemed more of a challenge. I welcomed it. The dash lights radiated a soft white luminance. The only sound was the low hum of the heater motors and the engine. The compass, awash in a faint green glow, was steady on a course of 285 degrees. It just doesn't get any better. Yesterday was work. Today was an adventure.

Rusty continued her snooze, but shifted it to her travel chair across from me.

Ahead, a triangle of bright lights drew closer. Five engines were pulling a long line of flatcars. Each car carried the back half of an eighteen-wheeler. It takes one man to run a truck, but only two or three to run a train carrying hundreds of trucks. As long as economics control the way we move things in this country, there will always be railroads. Just a thought in the dark. Another platitude on the road.

Encino and Willard had nothing open that sold coffee, but Mountainair did. The sun was just coming up as I drove through town. With 1,500 people, most involved in ranching,

Mountainair is the biggest town along here. It's ten miles off from being the geographic center of New Mexico.

The waitress in the Ancient Cities Café wore a green-and-black plaid shirt over her loose, pink uniform. She poured my coffee at the counter, then poured rounds for customers at the tables.

Four were local ranchers, hunched around a table, talking with little animation or expression. Two others were obviously tourists, a natty couple who talked not at all. They read a newspaper. The only new car outside, with a dealer's sticker from Dallas, was probably theirs. The lady wore tinted glasses attached to a silver leash that looped around her neck. It reminded me of a piece of yarn that my mother in Minnesota attached to my mittens so that I would not lose them.

The cook, in jeans and an apron, stepped out of the kitchen with a rack of clean coffee cups. She stacked them by a radio that played a country station "and always has," she added. Looking at my camera, she suggested I take pictures of the Shaffer Hotel and the train depot before I leave town.

"Everybody makes a fuss over the seventeenth-century Indian ruins we have around here, but I like the old things my ancestors built." She left for the kitchen to butter some English muffins, then came back. "You know the thing now is to pick up and move these old rural train depots and make shops or restaurants out of them for city people. Nobody will touch our depot," she insisted, smiling. "It's solid concrete."

The Shaffer Hotel, which opened in May of 1924, still has that classic, mature look of the twenties, if you can divorce it from the portable TV in the lobby. Just being there, even dark and silent, the idiot box jars the senses like graffiti. The lobby is small, as is the hotel. No one was at the desk or in the dining room.

The only people around were a couple speaking French who were recording the walls, furnishings, ceilings, everything with a video camera. They looked at the wooden stairs for the longest time. Then the man zoomed the camera into the corner of several steps. This was too much for my curiosity. Luckily, they spoke English and showed me what they had discovered.

Where each step meets the wall, a three-sided corner, a piece of wood, had been inserted. It's best described as a dished-out, inverted pyramid, which made the corner a curve. "Dust bunnies hide in corners," the lady said. "They cannot hide where there are no corners."

The train depot is now a workshop for the railroad workers. The windows were boarded up, but the doors were wide open. In front, an empty pickup truck with its driver's door open spoke loudly of railroad business up and down the line on a two-way radio. I saw no one around listening to it.

Mountainair started on this very spot in 1903 with the railroad. It brought the homesteaders. Like the Spanish settlers and Indians before them, the newcomers grew corn and beans. As the town grew, it took on the name "Pinto-Bean Capital of the World." The droughts of the late 1940s and 1950s caused most of the farms to be abandoned or sold. Today a livestock industry flourishes.

Back on Highway 60, the motorhome was almost coasting as I lost elevation coming off the Manzano Range. I dropped into neutral. The speedometer didn't move a notch. I remember doing the same thing months ago coming out of Borrego Springs, California. This time, however, I felt like I was drifting—no, more like being pushed—toward a finish line. It's always out there somewhere.

Ahead lay the Rio Grande River. In this dead expanse of brown, trees do not grow except along the river. There they flourish. Today they are a rich, gorgeous curtain of brilliant fall colors that extend across the earth, I am sure, from top to bottom.

Mexicans know the Rio Grande as the Rio Bravo, the "Wild River." Yet it is neither bravo nor grande right now. The riverbed is wide, room for more water than is in it. I can only guess what it was once, and may still be at a different time.

Maybe someday I'll come back and see for myself, God willing.

72

Street of Healing Magic

Truth or Consequences, New Mexico

The residents of San Francisco get upset when their swank city by the bay is called "Frisco." But down here, folks don't care if you shorten the name of their town. They all do. Everybody calls it "T or C," because "Truth or Consequences" is just too much.

"Better than half our incoming mail is addressed to T or C, New Mexico 87901. Some of it is still addressed to Hot Springs. If the zip is right, we get it," a clerk at the post office told me.

A few here, holdouts from four decades back, stubbornly persist that Hot Springs is their correct address. The school board may be the most die-hard holdouts of them all. The high school, to this day, is still Hot Springs High.

"This name always causes problems when I order things by phone," says Reyes Tenorio in Ron's Sporting Goods. "When I give my address, they don't believe me. They say, 'That can't be a town.' Then I have to go through the whole nine yards."

Truth or Consequences, the radio quiz show, started in 1940. Hosted by Ralph Edwards, it was a national hit and continued into the 1950s as a network TV show. In 1950,

Edwards announced that he would do his tenth-anniversary radio show from any town in the country that would change its name to Truth or Consequences. There were several takers. Edwards' choice was Hot Springs, New Mexico, a small town of ranchers, merchants, and mineral-water bathers. He liked the idea of the natural hot springs here, which were said to have benefited thousands who suffered from rheumatism and arthritis. Also, there was an orthopedic hospital for children here that interested him.

But the final decision lay with those who lived here. Many here asked, "Why take the silly name of a radio program and give up a name that is descriptive of what nature has given us? And all this for an hour in the national spotlight?" The other side argued, "Why not? The Hot Springs name is too common. Consider all the free publicity the town will get, now and forever." The vote came in 1,294 for, 295 against. On March 31, 1950, the name changed.

The next day, the first Truth or Consequences Fiesta was staged here. It brought 10,000 people into town. That evening, the Truth or Consequences show originated from its day-old namesake.

T or C still celebrates its fiesta every year, on the first weekend in May. Edwards is always here for it. He brings a celebrity or two to help draw a crowd and rides a horse in the annual parade. His relationship with this community is still very close. They named a riverside park after him a few years back.

The Geronimo Springs Museum, on Main Street, has a large room devoted to Edwards and his radio show. The photography and memorabilia cover his nearly fifty-year association with this town. Outside is a stone arch covering a pool of warm water bubbling up out of the ground. "Geronimo often stopped here to bathe and relax," the sign says. It lists nine bathhouses, with an invitation to visit them.

Ann Welborn has lived here all her life and runs the museum. She acknowledges that Edwards has helped the town, but everything considered, the name change has not accomplished what many thought it would. In fact, in 1964

and again in 1967, the question of whether to keep the name
went to a vote here. Though obviously controversial, the T or
C name still suits the majority.

"Some think we should have actively promoted the health
benefits of our natural hot springs and not just relied on
fallout from the Truth or Consequences thing. They did that
kind of promotion in the forties. People came from all over.
We were known as the 'city of health.' I don't suppose many
people think of us as that anymore.

"A local lady, she's dead now, Magnolia Ellis, was a
magnetic healer. There was something in her hands," Ann
recalls. "After she rubbed you, whatever was wrong got better. She used to treat 150 to 200 people a day. Can you
imagine?"

Apparently, the magnetic healer's hands may have also
rubbed a little cash. Walking down Broadway later, the business street, I noticed the two-story Magnolia Ellis Apartments.

The Indians of the Southwest considered the site of the
present town neutral ground. Here they gathered to bathe
their wounds and ailments and exchange tribal news. They
called it Geronimo Springs, after the Apache chief who was
possibly the greatest Indian military leader of the nineteenth
century.

Newcomer Shirley Hatfield, owner of the Marshall Miracle
Hot Springs, a bathhouse, would like to see this place again
be known as Geronimo Springs. "For a spot that has proven
powers of pain removal and healing, a name like T or C
makes no sense at all. It's become a joke. Some call the town
'Torc.' Hot Springs is a decent but overworked name.
Geronimo Springs says it all, without copying anybody."

A bunch of cowboys built the first bathhouse in 1882.
Later, when the county was formed, it built one. Today private enterprise has taken over the natural hot springs here.
Five privately owned bathhouses offer a couple of different
ways to soak in the 112-degree mineral water. You can soak
in a tub, emptied after each use. Or you can relax in a
cement-sided pool where the water percolates up through

gravel in the bottom and flows out through an overflow at the top.

Shirley claims her naturally flowing pools change water every thirty minutes, but that's a tough one to prove. She is a firm believer in the healing powers of the water. To make doubly sure, she had Longstanding Bear Chief come down from Montana to give her place a proper Native American blessing.

"We charge two dollars. That's for the towels and room. The water is free, as it should be. For many who come here, this is the end of the line, the end of the pain train. They must get something out of it. They keep coming back, even to the same pool every time. To them, it's theirs. To most, I'm just the sweeper here."

Off Broadway, in the dirt parking lot serving a row of dilapidated apartments, a sign reads Body Alignment. I half expected it to include breaks, shocks, struts and front-end work.

Across the street, a fancier sign on painted poles reads Better Health—Pressure-Point Relaxation—Special Food Balancing—By Appointment. Obviously, this is the street of healing magic, no questions asked, no guarantees, no license required.

On Marr Street, I joined a group of healthy-looking seniors sitting on the porch of the Artesian Bathhouse and RV Park. I got to talking with a nice couple from Rochester, Minnesota. Every year for the past ten, they have stopped here for a few days to and from their winter hangout in Yuma, Arizona.

"Oh, we love it!" the man said. "We get in the tub, exercise every muscle that works, and hop out feeling great."

"You're not here to cure anything?" I asked.

"Cure what? You know something I don't?" his wife laughed.

The man's wide grin raised his glasses from his nose. "I know what you are getting at. No, hot water, even in a backyard spa, is a great relaxer and pain dispenser, best taken with a glass of bourbon."

"Believe me, if the water bubbling out of this ground cures anything, the Mayo Clinic would have a glass-brick building over where we now sit. But look around. What do you see?"

I shook my head.

"That's right," he said, as he and his wife go in to soak.

73

The True Journey Never Ends

Deming, New Mexico

Jack Nicklaus said it best: "The older you get, the stronger
the wind gets, and it's always in your face."

These words have real meaning for me today. I am feeling it all, especially as it applies to getting older.

This is Deming, New Mexico. The wind is not only strong,
it is ferocious. When I did the hookup ritual, it was in my face
no matter what direction I turned. What's more, I have just
been jolted into reality. Seven months have passed since I
began this journey, and I have not really thought much about
the passage of time. How long can I keep this up? How long
should I?

It happened just now when I filled the motorhome with
gas. I went to record the pertinent numbers in my logbook
and found there was no more room. It has taken over two
years to do it and about 40,000 miles, but I have used every
line on every page. Am I being told that my journey has
ended? Well, I am not ready to end it.

Flipping through the dog-eared pages of the log, every
entry triggers a memory. People. Events. Places. Times.
Memorable days. Sure, some have not been so great. But they
have been my best yet—the good and the bad alike—because

I have lived every one of them to the hilt. They are all remarkably clear now, as if they happened just the other day.

You may call them yesterdays. But yesterday has a special meaning out here. Drifters. Adventurers. Explorers. Escapees. We nomads who don't stay still long. We live our lives in the here and now. What you see is what we are. What we were, or might have been, is of no consequence or interest to anyone. It just doesn't matter. There are no yesterdays on the road.

The person who hangs onto yesterday, who needs it for his survival today, is not out here with us. He spends his days seeking sameness and uniformity to release him from uncertainty and turmoil. I pity him, the man concealed by his own life, pursuing the status quo, scared to move, perhaps holding himself too closely. I know the feeling. I have been there.

Those of us who are out here searching, for whatever it may be, all have yesterdays that we treasure and some haunting ones we try to forget. But it is not where we live. We take our joy in the present, even revel in it, maybe too much so. But it is every bit the journey and the property of those who make it. It is the great equalizer. No, there are no yesterdays on the road.

Tonight, Rusty and I will stay here, undoubtedly rocked to sleep by the wind. Then we will head into Arizona and visit Tombstone. I have never been to Tombstone. I want to see the OK Corral and walk around town. I am curious about that place. We will do that tomorrow, unless something comes up that's more interesting.

About the Author

Bill Graves became a travel writer in the late 80s, covering the Western United States in his motorhome. His column, "America's Outback," appears monthly in *Trailer Life Magazine*. He's also written articles for numerous newspapers, including *The Chicago Tribune, The San Diego Union,* and *Long Beach Press-Telegram*. His work has also appeared in *Westways, Retired Officer,* and *Motorhome* magazines.

Graves spent ten years working in the Hollywood film and television industry as a military technical advisor on such films as *The Winds of War* and *An Officer and a Gentleman*. A retired Navy captain, Graves served twenty-four years as a public affairs officer; his Navy career also included two tours in Vietnam between 1965 and 1969.

A native of Minnesota, Graves is a graduate of the University of Minnesota. Today, when he is not traveling in his motorhome, he makes his home in Palos Verdes, California. Graves has two grown children who also live in Southern California.

The author invites your comments by email at:.

Roadscribe@aol.com

On the Back Roads — *Discovering Small Towns of America* Bill Graves / 1-886039-36-4	*$16.95*
The ABCs of Gold Investing Michael Kosares / 1-886039-29-1	*$14.95*
Battle at Alcatraz — *A Desperate Attempt to Escape the Rock* Ernest Lageson / 1-886039-37-2	*$16.95*
Counterpoint — A Murder in Massachusetts Bay Margaret Press / 1-886039-24-0	*16.95*
Eye of the Beast Terry Adams / 1-886039	*16.95*
The Family Compatibility Test Susan Adams / 1-886039-27-5	*$9.95*
First Impressions — Tips to Enhance Your Image Joni Craighead / 1-886039-26-7	*$14.95*

The Healing Touch—Keeping the Doctor/Patient
   Relationship Alive Under Managed Care
   David Cram, MD / 1-886039-31-3
	$9.95

Hello, Methuselah! Living to 100 and Beyond George Webster, PhD / 1-886039-25-9	*$14.95*
Prescription Drug Abuse — The Hidden Epidemic Rod Colvin / 1-886039-22-4	*$14.95*
Simple Changes: *The Boomer's Guide to a Healthier, Happier Life* L. Joe Porter, MD / 1-886039-35-6	*$9.95*
Straight Talk About Breast Cancer Suzanne Braddock, MD / 1-886039-21-6	*$12.95*
The Street-Smart Entrepreneur Jay Goltz / 1-886039-33-X	*$14.95*
The Stroke Recovery Book Kip Burkman, MD / 1-886039-30-5	*$14.95*
Suddenly Gone Dan Mitrione / 1-886039-23-2	*$15.95*
Understanding Postpartum Depression and Anxiety Linda Sebastian, RN / 1-886930-34-8	*$12.95*

Please send:

_____ copies of _____
                          (*Title of book*)

at $_____ each   TOTAL   _____

Nebr. residents add 5% sales tax   _____

Shipping/Handling
    $3.00 for first book.
    $1.00 for each additional book.   _____

            TOTAL ENCLOSED   _____

Name_____

Address_____

City _____ State_____ Zip _____

☐ Visa   ☐ Master Card   ☐ Am. Express

Credit card number _____

Expiration date _____

Order by credit card, personal check or money order.

Send to:

Addicus Books
Mail Order Dept.
P.O. Box 45327
Omaha, NE 68145
Or, order **TOLL FREE: 800-352-2873**

Please send:

_____ copies of _____

(*Title of book*)

at $_____each   TOTAL   _____

Nebr. residents add 5% sales tax   _____

Shipping/Handling
    $3.00 for first book.
    $1.00 for each additional book.   _____

    TOTAL ENCLOSED   _____

Name _____

Address _____

City _____ State _____ Zip _____

☐ Visa   ☐ Master Card   ☐ Am. Express

Credit card number _____

Expiration date _____

Order by credit card, personal check or money order.

Send to:

Addicus Books
Mail Order Dept.
P.O. Box 45327
Omaha, NE 68145
Or, order **TOLL FREE: 800-352-2873**